Favorite Timeless Patterns
for Today's Quilter

by The Editors of *Traditional Quiltworks* and *Quilting Today* magazines

CHITRA PUBLICATIONS

Your Best Value in Quilting!

Copyright ©1999
All Rights Reserved. Published in the United States of America
Printed in Hong Kong
Chitra Publications
2 Public Avenue
Montrose, Pennsylvania 18801-1220

No part of this publication may be reproduced or transmitted in any form or by any means, electronic or mechanical, including photocopy, recording, or any information storage and retrieval system now known or to be invented, without permission in writing from the publisher, except by a reviewer who wishes to quote brief passages in connection with a review written for inclusion in a magazine, newspaper, or broadcast.

First printing: 1999
Library of Congress Cataloging-in-Publication Data

Favorite timeless patterns for today's quilter/from the editors of Traditional quiltworks and Quilting today.
p.cm.
ISBN 1-885588-31-3
1. Patchwork—Patterns.   2. Appliqué—Patterns.   3. Quilts
TT835 .F387 1999
746.46'041—dc21   99-050360

Edited by: Debra Feece
Design & Illustration: Kimberly Steele
Cover Photography: Guy Cali Associates, Clarks Summit, PA
Inside Photography: VanZandbergen Photography, Brackney, PA and Stephen J. Appel, Vestal, NY

Our Mission Statement

We publish quality quilting magazines and books that recognize, promote and inspire self-expression. We are dedicated to serving our customers with respect, kindness and efficiency.

The editorial team—clockwise from the top: Jack Braunstein, Debra Feece, Debbie Hearn, Elsie Campbell and Joyce Libal

---

From the moment you turn the first page, you'll be glad you chose this pattern book. It holds the key to some wonderful family heirlooms you can begin stitching today. All of the classic patterns on the pages that follow are included not only for their traditional charm, but also to provide you with variety in design and construction techniques. Many of the quilts are scrappy, so all of you fabric lovers (and what quilter isn't?) will have the pleasure of combining lots of fabrics in plenty of fun ways. These quilts are among our favorites from past issues of *Traditional Quiltworks* and *Quilting Today* magazines.

If piecing is your forté, you'll revel in making quilts like "Wheel of Fortune" and "Plaid Stars, Rolling Stars." The first features strip-pieced, checkerboard sashing. The latter is accented with pieced stars in the sashing and a unique streak o' lightning border. Fans of no-template methods will find a fine starting place in "Plaid Paws," a Bear's Paw quilt made with deep-tone plaids, "Star Within a Star," or "Diamond Log Cabin" with its red plaid block centers and pieced "brick" border.

These quilts span the seasons. Be ready for the holidays when you display your own version of "Christmas Ivy," festive with assorted red prints and attractive diamond border. It's easy to make with no-template sewing. Welcome spring with "Magnolia," a pieced flower quilt in a "strippy" setting. It's softened with a graceful scalloped edge.

In the something-for-everyone tradition, we've also included "Bluebird of Happiness." This exuberant medallion quilt has a folk-art appliqué center surrounded by three borders—sawtooth, floral appliqué and pieced stars. Rather than piecing the hundreds of hexagons required for a Grandmother's Flower Garden quilt, make "Posies." You piece just seven hexagons for each of the flowers in this design. Then appliqué each flower to a background square along with leaves and stems. Set the blocks on point and sash them for a flower quilt the easy way!

Piecing and simple appliqué are also combined in "Postage Stamp Basket," a quilt reminiscent of the folk-art commemorative U.S. stamp which honored the timeless art of quilting. Last but not least, appliqué the classic red-and-green "President's Wreath." You need only a few pattern pieces, but the look is truly elegant.

Where will you begin? Page through the book and let the color photos inspire you! Then create timeless treasures for your family and friends to enjoy for generations. Happy stitching from the editors of *Traditional Quiltworks* and *Quilting Today*.

Contents

General Directions 32

Patterns

Wheel of Fortune 4

Christmas Ivy 6

Diamond Log Cabin 8

Plaid Paws 10

President's Wreath 12

Star Within a Star 15

Posies 16

Magnolia 19

Plaid Stars, Rolling Stars 20

Postage Stamp Basket 23

Bluebird of Happiness 25

Pattern Ratings
Beginner   Intermediate   Advanced

Wheel of Fortune

Stitch a bit of timeless beauty!

*Checkerboard sashing adds casual grace to this antique **"Wheel of Fortune"** quilt (67 1/2" x 84") from the collection of publisher, Christiane Meunier. A single bright green block provides an energetic focal point—cover the block and see how "quiet" the quilt becomes!*

QUILT SIZE: 69" x 83 1/2"
BLOCK SIZE: 10" square

MATERIALS
Yardage is estimated for 44" fabric.
- Scraps of dark prints, or 15 different 1/4 yard pieces
- 3 3/4 yards muslin
- 1 3/4 yards pink print
- 5 yards backing fabric
- 73" x 88" piece of batting

CUTTING
Pattern pieces are full size and include a 1/4" seam allowance, as do all dimensions given. We recommend making a sample block before cutting fabric for the entire quilt.

For each of 30 blocks:
- Cut 1: A, dark print
- Cut 16: B, same dark print; or cut four 3 1/2" squares, then cut them in quarters diagonally
- Cut 4: D, same dark print; or cut two 3 7/8" squares, then cut them in half diagonally

Also:
- Cut 480: B, muslin; or cut one hundred twenty 3 1/2" squares, then cut them in quarters diagonally
- Cut 240: C, muslin
- Cut 18: 2" x 44" strips, muslin
- Cut 30: 2" x 44" strips, pink print
- Cut 8: 2 1/2" x 44" strips, pink print, for the binding

PIECING
For each block:
- Sew 4 muslin B's to a dark print A, as shown, to make a block center.

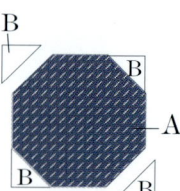

- Sew a dark print B to a muslin B to make a pieced triangle. Make 8.

- Join 2 pieced triangles to make a pieced square. Make 4.
- Sew a muslin C to opposite sides of a pieced square, as shown. Sew dark print B's to the unit to complete a side unit. Make 4.

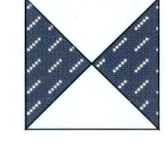

- Stitch a muslin B to each end of 2 side units. Lay out the units, as shown. Sew them together.

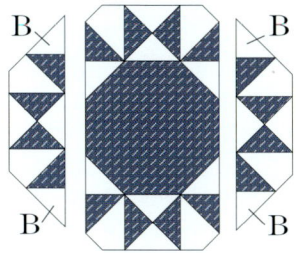

- Sew a dark print D to each corner to complete a Wheel of Fortune block. Make 30. Set them aside.

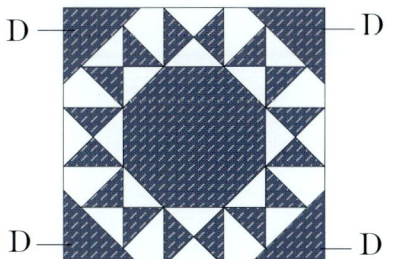

- Stitch a 2" x 44" muslin strip between two 2" x 44" pink print strips, along their length, to make a pieced strip. Make 14. Press the seam allowances toward the pink print. From one of the pieced strips, cut twenty 2" slices, as shown. Set the remaining pieced strips aside.
- Sew a 2" x 44" pink print strip between two 2" x 44" muslin strips. Make 2. Press the seam allowances toward the pink print.

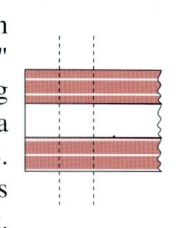

Cut forty 2" slices from the pieced strips.
- Lay out three 2" slices, as shown. Join them to make a Nine Patch block. Make 20.
- From the remaining pieced strips, cut forty-nine 10 1/2" sashing strips.

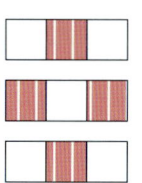

ASSEMBLY
- Lay out 5 sashing strips and 4 Nine Patch blocks. Stitch them together, alternating sashing strips and Nine Patches, to make a sashing row. Make 5.
- Referring to the quilt photo, lay out the blocks in 6 rows of 5. Place sashing strips between the blocks in each horizontal row. Place the sashing rows between the rows of blocks.
- Join the blocks and sashing strips in each horizontal row. Join the rows.
- Finish the quilt as described in the *General Directions,* using the 2 1/2" x 44" pink print strips for the binding.

Full-Size Pattern Pieces for Wheel of Fortune

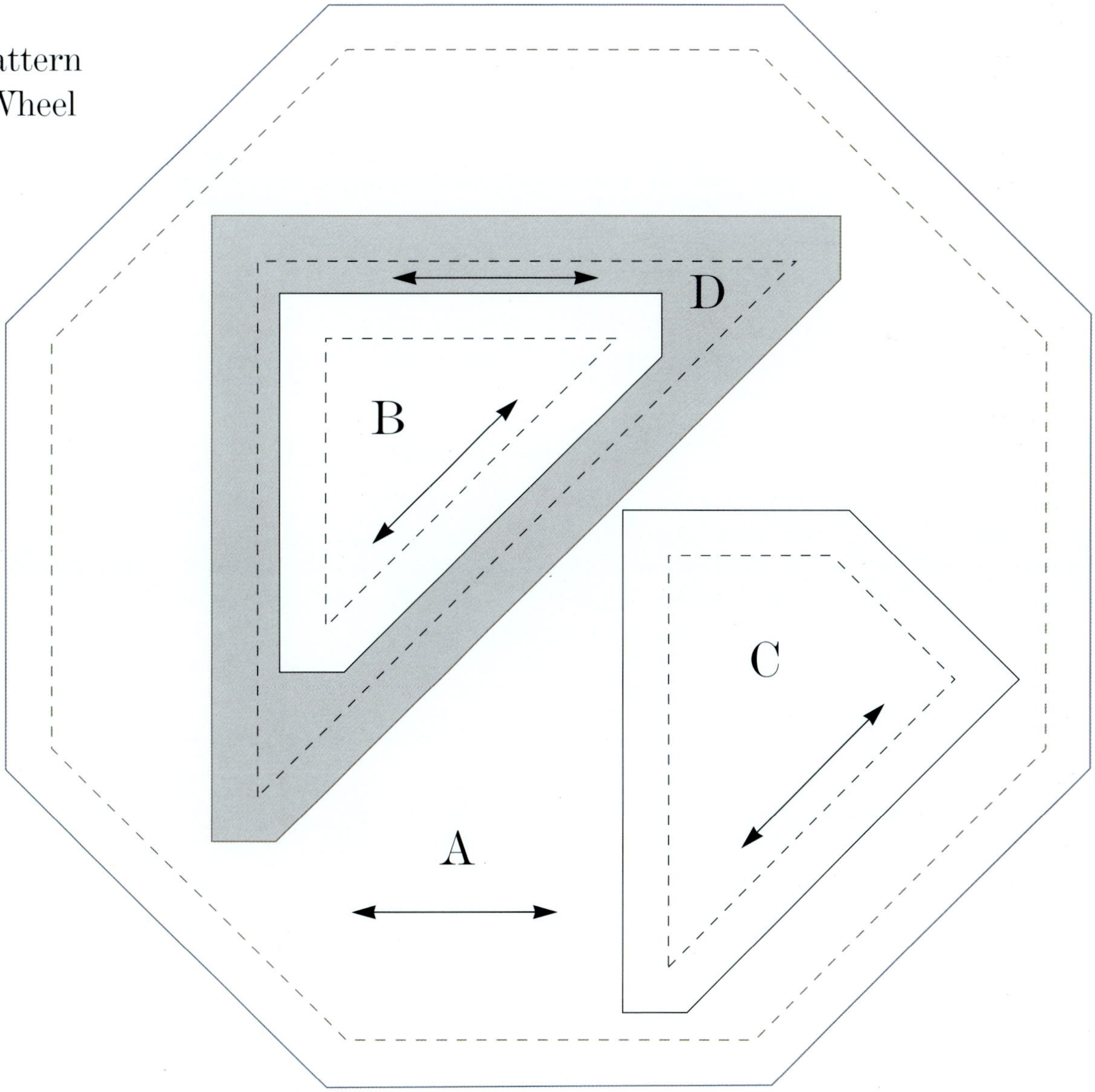

Christmas Ivy

by Lyn Mann

Make a festive quilt to decorate your home for the holidays

QUILT SIZE: 67 1/2" x 84 1/2"
BLOCK SIZE: 12" square

MATERIALS
Yardage is estimated for 44" fabric.
- Assorted red prints totaling 2 1/2 yards
- Assorted light green prints totaling 3/4 yard
- Assorted dark green prints totaling 1 yard
- Assorted beige prints totaling 4 yards
- 2 1/2 yards red print for the outer border and binding
- 5 yards backing fabric
- 72" x 89" piece of batting

CUTTING
Dimensions include a 1/4" seam allowance. Cut the lengthwise binding and border strips parallel to the selvage before cutting other pieces from the red print fabric. We recommend making a sample block before cutting fabric for the entire quilt.

For each of 12 Ivy Units:
- Cut 1: 2 1/2" square, light green print
- Cut 1: 2 7/8" square, light green print, then cut it in half diagonally
- Cut 1: 3 7/8" square, beige print, then cut it in half diagonally to yield 2 triangles. Label them C.
- Cut 1: 3 1/2" square, same beige print, then cut it in half diagonally to yield 2 triangles. Label them B.
- Cut 6: 1 7/8" squares, same beige print, then cut them in half diagonally to yield 12 triangles. You will use 11. Label them A.
- Cut 5: 1 7/8" squares, one dark green print, then cut them in half diagonally to yield 10 triangles. You will use 9.
- Cut 1: 2" square, same dark green print
- Cut 1: 1" x 5" strip, same dark green print

For each of 72 Snow Crystals:
NOTE: *Group the red print pieces and beige print pieces for each unit as you cut them.*

- Cut 3: 2" squares, one red print
- Cut 3: 2 3/8" squares, same red print, then cut them in half diagonally
- Cut 3: 2" squares, one beige print
- Cut 3: 2 3/8" squares, same beige print, then cut them in half diagonally. Label them D.

For the pieced border:
- Cut 60: 3 1/2" squares, assorted light and dark green prints
- Cut 14: 5 1/2" squares, assorted beige prints, then cut them in quarters diagonally. Label them E.
- Cut 14: 5 1/2" squares, red border print, then cut them in quarters diagonally to yield 56 small triangles
- Cut 2: 5 1/8" squares, red border print, then cut them in half diagonally to yield 4 large triangles

Also:
- Cut 6: 6 1/2" squares, assorted beige prints
- Cut 3: 18 1/4" squares, assorted beige prints, then cut them in quarters diagonally to yield 12 setting triangles. You will use 10.
- Cut 2: 9 3/8" squares, beige prints, then cut them in half diagonally to yield 4 corner triangles
- Cut 4: 2 1/2" x 88" lengthwise strips, red print, for the binding
- Cut 2: 4 1/4" x 78" lengthwise strips, red print, for the outer border
- Cut 2: 4 1/4" x 70" lengthwise strips, red print, for the outer border

DIRECTIONS
For each of 12 Ivy Units:
- Sew a beige print triangle A to a dark green print triangle to make a pieced square. Make 9.

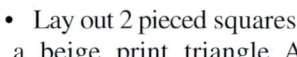

- Lay out 5 pieced squares and the 2 1/2" light green print square. Sew the pieced squares into sections, as shown. Sew them to the square to

make Unit 1. Set it aside.
- Lay out 2 pieced squares, a beige print triangle A and a light green print triangle. Join the pieced squares and the beige print triangle. Sew the section to the light green print triangle to make a pieced section, as shown.

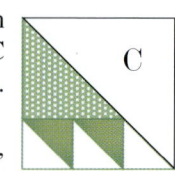

- Sew the pieced section to a beige print triangle C to make Unit 2, as shown. Set it aside.
- Lay out 2 pieced squares, a beige print triangle A and a light green print triangle. Join the pieced squares and the beige print triangle. Sew this section to the light green print triangle to make a pieced section, as shown.
- Sew the pieced section to a beige print triangle C to make Unit 3, as shown. Set is aside.
- Center and sew a 1" x 5" dark green print strip between 2 beige print triangle B's to make a stem section, as shown. Square the corners.

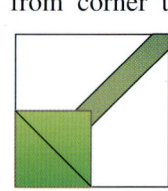

- Draw a diagonal line from corner to corner, on the wrong side of a 2" dark green square. Lay the square on the stem section, right sides together, as shown. Sew on the drawn line.
- Press the dark green piece open and trim the seam allowance to 1/4". This is Unit 4.
- Lay out Units 1 through 4. Join them to complete an Ivy Unit, as shown.

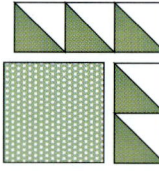

For each of 72 Snow Crystals:
- Sew a red print triangle to a beige print triangle D to make a pieced square. Make 6.
- Lay out 2 pieced squares, a 2" red print square and a 2" beige print square. Join them to make a section, as shown. Make 3.

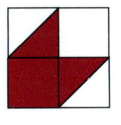

NOTE: *Each Snow Crystal is made up of 3 matching sections. Group the sections as you make them. Make 72 groups.*
- Lay out an Ivy Unit and 4 groups of matching Snow Crystal sections.
- Join the sections, as shown. Sew them to the Ivy Unit to complete a Christmas Ivy block. Make 12.

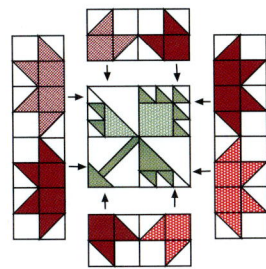

- In the same manner, but using a 6 1/2" beige print square in place of the Ivy Unit, make an alternate block, as shown. Make 6.

- Referring to the quilt photo, lay out the Christmas Ivy blocks, alternate blocks, setting triangles and beige print corner triangles. Sew the blocks and triangles into diagonal rows and join the rows.

For the pieced border:
- Sew 2 beige print triangle E's to a 3 1/2" green print square to make an end unit, as shown. Make 4. Set them aside.

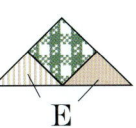

- Sew a small red border print triangle and a beige print triangle E to a 3 1/2" green print square to make a pieced unit, as shown. Make 48.

- Join 10 pieced units to make a short border. Sew an end unit to the right end of

the short border. Make 2.
- Join 14 pieced units to make a long border. Sew an end unit to the right end of the long border. Make 2.
- Sew the short borders to the short sides of the quilt keeping the beige print triangles against the quilt.
- Sew the long borders to the long sides of the quilt in the same manner.
- Lay out two 3 1/2" green print squares and 2 small red border print triangles. Join them, as shown. 
- Sew a large red border print triangle to the pieced unit to make a corner unit,

as shown. Make 4.
- Sew a corner unit to each corner, referring to the photo as necessary.
- Measure the length of the quilt. Trim the 4 1/4" x 78" red print border strips to that measurement. Sew them to the long sides of the quilt.
- Measure the width of the quilt, including the borders. Trim the 4 1/4" x 70" red print border strips to that measurement. Sew them to the remaining sides of the quilt.
- Finish the quilt as described in the *General Directions,* using the 2 1/2" x 88" red print strips for the binding.

Lyn Mann of Lake Forest, California, says her favorite quilts are scrappy and the more fabrics used, the better! She designed **"Christmas Ivy"** *(67 1/2" x 84 1/2") and stitched it using a wide variety of green and red prints. It was machine quilted by Paula Reid of Palmdale, California.*

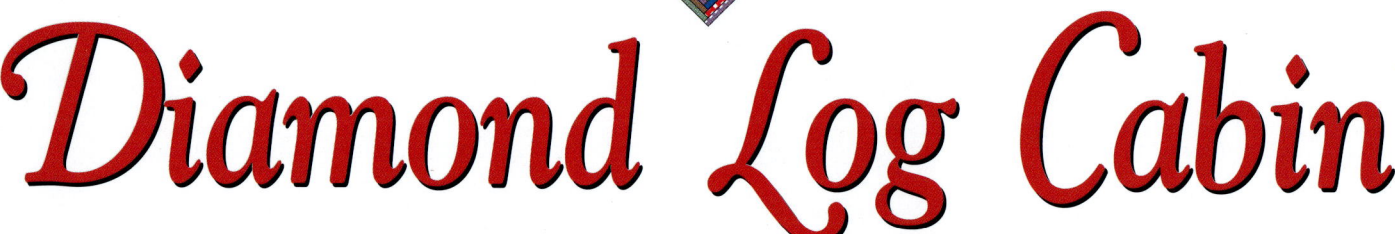

Diamond Log Cabin

Build a beautiful Log Cabin for yourself or someone special!

QUILT SIZE: 56 1/2" x 79 1/2"
BLOCK SIZE: 11 1/2" square

MATERIALS
Yardage is estimated for 44" fabric.
- Assorted dark prints and plaids totaling at least 2 2/3 yards, for the logs and outer border
- Assorted light prints totaling at least 2 yards, for the logs
- 1 yard red plaid, for the block centers and binding
- 1/4 yard dark blue print, for the inner border
- 4 1/2 yards of backing fabric
- 61" x 84" piece of batting

CUTTING
Dimensions include a 1/4" seam allowance.
- Cut 6: 1 1/2" x 13" strips, assorted dark prints
- Cut 80: 1 1/2" x 22" strips, assorted dark prints
- Cut 92: 2 1/2" x 6 1/2" strips, assorted dark prints, for the outer border
- Cut 90: 1 1/2" x 22" strips, assorted light prints, for the logs
- Cut 24: 2" squares, red plaid, for the block centers
- Cut 7: 2 1/2" x 44" strips, red plaid, for the binding
- Cut 6: 1 1/4" x 44" strips, dark blue print, for the inner border

PIECING
For 24 Log Cabin blocks: 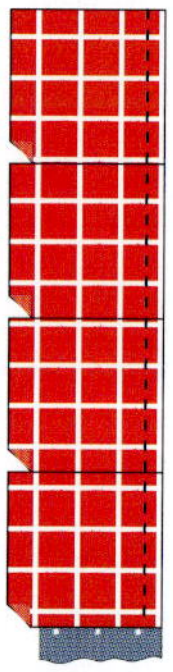
- Sew four 2" red squares one after another to a 1 1/2" x 13" dark print strip, as shown. Make 6.
- Cut the dark print strip between the squares and after the last square sewn. Press the seam allowances toward the dark print. Stack the units right side down, with the dark strip toward the bottom. 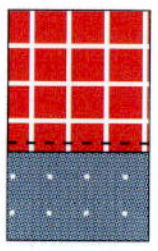
- In the same manner, sew the pieced units to a dark print strip, one after another, as shown.

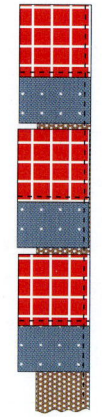

- Cut them apart, as before. Stack them right side down, with the last strip added toward the bottom.
- Sew the pieced units to a 1 1/2" x 44" light print strip, one after another. Cut them apart. Stack them with the last strip added toward the bottom.
- In the same manner, sew the pieced units to a light print strip, one after another. This completes Round 1.

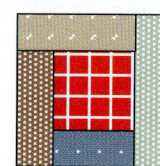

- Continue in this manner, sewing 1 1/2"-wide strips to the pieced units, alternating 2 light print strips with 2 dark print strips for each round until you have completed 5 rounds for each of 24 Log Cabin blocks.

ASSEMBLY
- Referring to the quilt photo, lay out the Log Cabin blocks in 6 rows of 4.
- Stitch the blocks into rows and join the rows.
- Stitch the six 1 1/4" x 44" dark blue print strips together, end to end, to make a pieced strip.
- Cut two 69 1/2" lengths from the pieced strip. Sew them to the long sides of the quilt.
- Cut two 48" lengths from the pieced strip. Sew them to the remaining sides of the quilt.
- Sew eight 2 1/2" x 6 1/2" dark print strips together, end to end, to make an outer pieced strip. Trim 1/4" from each end. Make 2.
- Sew nine 2 1/2" x 6 1/2" dark print strips, end to end. Trim 3 1/4" from each end, to make an inner pieced strip. Make 2.
- Offsetting the seams, as shown, stitch an outer and an inner pieced strip together along their length, to make a short pieced border. Make 2.

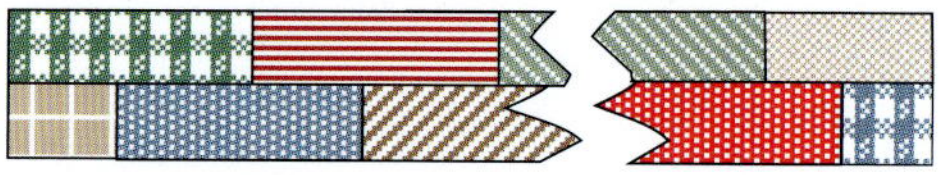

- Sew the short pieced borders to the short sides of the quilt with the inner pieced strip toward the quilt.
- Sew fourteen 2 1/2" x 6 1/2" dark print strips, end to end, to make a outer pieced strip. Make 2.
- Sew fifteen 2 1/2" x 6 1/2" dark print strips, end to end. Trim 3 1/4" from each end, to make an inner pieced strip. Make 2.
- Stitch an outer and an inner pieced strip together, offsetting the seams, to make a long pieced border. Make 2.
- Measure the length of the quilt. Trim the two long pieced borders to that measurement, trimming equal lengths from each end. Sew them to the long sides of the quilt.
- Finish the quilt as described in *General Directions*, using the 2 1/2" x 44" red plaid strips for the binding.

*Kathy Stewart of Clackamas, Oregon, built her **"Log Cabin"** (56 1/2" x 79 12") using bunches of scraps. Kathy has made many Log Cabin quilts, but the unusual diamond set makes this quilt her favorite!*

Plaid Paws

Tame your wild plaids with a simple setting and border.

QUILT SIZE: 89 1/2" x 107 1/2"
BLOCK SIZE: 10 1/2" square

MATERIALS

Yardage is estimated for 44" fabric.
- Assorted dark plaids totaling at least 2 3/4 yards
- Assorted light plaids totaling at least 2 3/4 yards
- 1/3 yard red plaid
- 3 yards second red plaid
- 4 yards dark green print
- 1 3/4 yards tan plaid
- 8 yards backing fabric
- 94" x 112" piece of batting

CUTTING

Dimensions include a 1/4" seam allowance. Cut the lengthwise dark green print border strips before cutting smaller pieces from that fabric.

For each of 32 blocks:
- Cut 8: 2 3/8" squares, dark plaid
- Cut 1: 2" square, same dark plaid
- Cut 4: 3 1/2" squares, second dark plaid
- Cut 4: 2" squares, light plaid
- Cut 8: 2 3/8" squares, same light plaid
- Cut 4: 2" x 5" strips, same light plaid

For the 4 border paw units:
- Cut 8: 2 3/8" squares, dark plaid
- Cut 4: 3 1/2" squares, second dark plaid
- Cut 4: 2" squares, light plaid
- Cut 8: 2 3/8" squares, same light plaid

Also:
- Cut 49: 2 1/4" squares, red plaid, for the cornerstones
- Cut 4: 3" squares, red plaid, for the inner border
- Cut 2: 10 7/8" squares, light tan plaid, then cut them in half diagonally to yield 4 corner triangles
- Cut 4: 18 5/8" squares, light tan plaid, then cut them in quarters diagonally to yield 16 setting traingles. You will use 14.
- Cut 4: 5" x 102" strips, second red plaid, for the outer borders
- Cut 4: 3" x 97" strips, dark green print, for the inner borders
- Cut 80: 2 1/4" x 11" strips, dark green print, for the sashing
- Cut 12: 2 1/2" x 44" strips, dark green print, for the binding

DIRECTIONS

For each of 32 blocks:
- Draw a diagonal line from corner to corner on the wrong side of 8 matching 2 3/8" light plaid squares.
- Lay a marked light plaid square on a 2 3/8" dark plaid square, right sides together, and sew 1/4" away from the diagonal line on both sides. Make 8.
- Cut the squares apart on the marked lines to yield 16 pieced squares.
- Join 2 pieced squares facing in one direction and 2 pieced squares facing in the opposite direction, as shown, to form pieced strips.

- Sew one of the pieced strips to a 3 1/2" second dark plaid square, as shown.

- Sew a 2" light plaid square to the remaining pieced strip, and use it to complete a paw unit, as shown. Make 4.

- Sew a 2" x 5" light plaid strip between 2 paw units, as shown. Make 2.

- Sew the 2" dark plaid square between the 2 remaining 2" x 5" light plaid strips, to form the block's center strip.
- Use the center strip to complete a Bear's Paw block, as shown. Make 32. Set them aside.

- Construct 4 paw units to be used in the border. Set them aside.

ASSEMBLY

- Sew a 2 1/4" red plaid square to one end of a 2 1/4" x 11" dark green print strip to make a pieced strip. Make 40. Set 2 aside.
- Join 3 pieced strips end to end to make a pieced sashing. Make 2. In the same manner make 2 pieced sashings using 5 pieced strips for each, 2 pieced sashings using 7 pieced strips for each, and one pieced sashing using 8 pieced strips.
- Sew a 2 1/4" red plaid square to the end of each pieced sashing and the 2 pieced strips you set aside, so they all begin and end with a red plaid square.
- Lay out the blocks in diagonal rows, with 2 1/4" x 11" dark green print strips between the blocks and pieced sashing strips between the rows, referring to the quilt photo as necessary.
- Lay out the setting triangles and corner triangles to complete the rows.
- Sew the blocks, 2 1/4" x 11" sashing strips and setting triangles into diagonal rows.
- Join the rows and pieced sashing strips.

*Jayne Turner, of Ottawa, Kansas, collected enough dark plaids for at least four quilts while searching for the variety she desired for **"Plaid Paws"** (89 1/2" x 107 1/2"). Use all of your favorites in this scrappy, country-style quilt.*

- Sew the corner triangles to the corners of the quilt.
- Measure the length of the quilt. Trim two 3" x 97" dark green print strips to that measurement. Set them aside.
- Measure the width of the quilt. Trim the remaining 3" x 97" dark green print strips to that measurement and sew them to the top and bottom of the quilt.
- Sew a trimmed strip between two 3" red plaid squares to make a pieced border strip. Make 2.
- Sew them to the long sides of the quilt.
- Measure the length of the quilt. Trim two 5" x 102" second red plaid strips to that measurement. Set them aside.
- Measure the width of the quilt. Trim the remaining 5" x 102" second red plaid strips to that measurement and sew them to the top and bottom of the quilt.
- Sew a trimmed strip between 2 paw units to make a pieced border strip, referring to the quilt photo as necessary. Make 2.
- Sew them to the long sides of the quilt.
- Finish the quilt as described in the *General Directions*, using the 2 1/2" x 44" dark green print strips for the binding.

President's Wreath

Reproduce this wonderful antique quilt.

QUILT SIZE: 73" x 87"
BLOCK SIZE: 23" square

MATERIALS
Yardage is estimated for 44" fabric.
- 4 1/4 yards muslin
- 2 5/8 yards red
- 2 3/4 yards green
- 1/8 yard yellow
- 5 1/8 yards backing fabric
- 77" x 91" piece of thin batting
- Piece of paper at least 24 1/2" square
- Dark marker

CUTTING
Appliqué pieces on page 14 are full size and do not include a seam allowance. Make templates for each of the pattern pieces and cut them out. Trace around the templates on the right side of the fabric and add a 1/8" to 3/16" turn-under allowance when cutting the pieces out. All other dimensions include a 1/4" seam allowance. Cut lengthwise strips parallel to the selvage before cutting other pieces from the same yardage.

For the appliqué:
- Cut 24: A, red
- Cut 48: B, red
- Cut 11: F, red
- Cut 8: 1" x 32" bias strips, green
- Cut 2: 1" x 29" crosswise strips, green
- Cut 24: C, green
- Cut 178: D, green
- Cut 24: E, yellow
- Cut 11: G, yellow

Also:
- Cut 6: 24 1/2" squares, muslin
- Cut 2: 3 1/2" x 77" strips, muslin, for the middle border
- Cut 2: 3 1/2" x 91" strips, muslin, for the middle border
- Cut 1: 9 1/2" x 70" strip, muslin, for the center panel
- Cut 4: 2 1/2" x 90" strips, red, for the binding
- Cut 2: 2 1/2" x 91" strips, red, for the inner border
- Cut 2: 2 1/2" x 77" strips, red, for the inner border
- Cut 2: 4 1/2" x 77" strips, green, for the outer border
- Cut 2: 4 1/2" x 91" strips, green, for the outer border

PREPARATION
- Fold a 24 1/2" square of paper in half, then in half again. Open the square. Using a pencil, center and trace template A on each fold line, 2 1/4" from the edge of the paper.

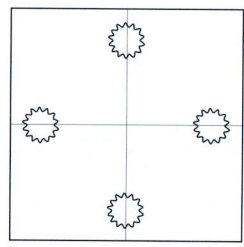

- Connect the flowers with a curved line to make a circle. Center and trace template C between the flowers. Trace template B at each end of the C's. Trace the D's, referring to the quilt photo for placement.

- When you are happy with the block drawing, trace the design with a dark marker.
- Place a 24 1/2" muslin square on the paper pattern. With a pencil, lightly trace the design on the muslin. Repeat for the remaining 24 1/2" muslin squares. Set them aside.
- Press each long edge of a 32" green bias strip 1/4" to the wrong side. Trim the allowances to 1/8" to reduce bulk. Cut three 10" strips from each pressed bias strip. These are the stems for the blocks.
- In the same manner, prepare the 1" x 29" green strips. Cut six 4 1/2" strips from each pressed strip. These are the stems for the center panel.

APPLIQUÉ DIRECTIONS
For each of 6 blocks:
- Using the drawn lines for placement, appliqué four 10" green bias stems to the muslin square.
- Use the tip of your needle to turn under the allowance as you appliqué the remaining pieces for each block. There is no need to turn under the allowance where pieces overlap.
- Appliqué the pieces in the following order:
  Red A's
  Red B's
  Green C's
  Green D's

QUILTING DESIGN SAMPLE FOR PRESIDENT'S WREATH

"President's Wreath" (73" x 87") *is a lovely antique owned by Barbara Trudeau of East Syracuse, New York. Barbara's mentor, Edith R. Gowing, hand appliquéd the quilt top for her only son in 1922, the year he was born. For only $5, the quilting was done by a woman from Tifton, Georgia, who was famed for her exquisite stitching. She closely quilted the background with hearts and small circles, some only the size of a dime.*

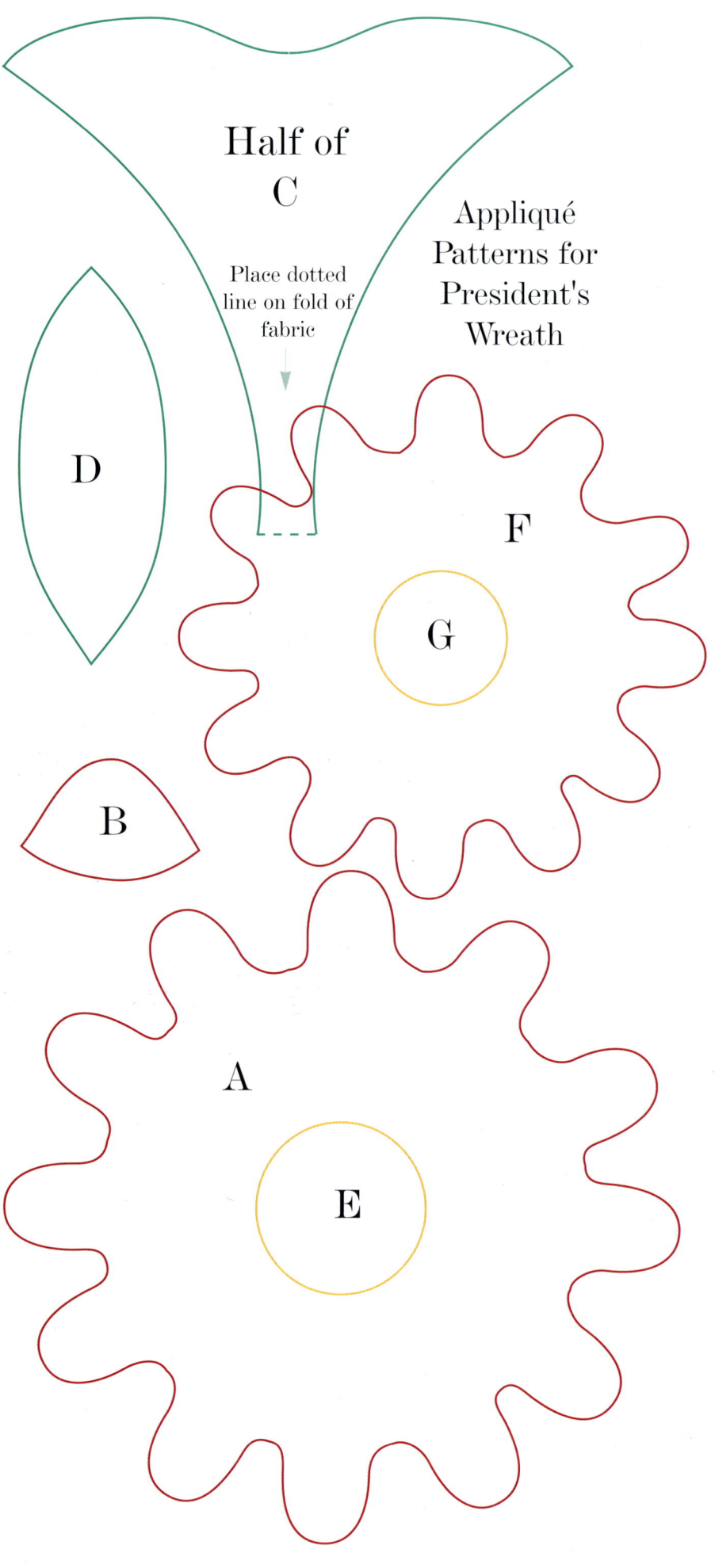

Appliqué Patterns for President's Wreath

Yellow E's
- Trim each block to 23 1/2" square, keeping the appliqué centered in the square.
- Sew 3 blocks together in a row. Make 2. Set them aside.
- Fold the 9 1/2" x 70" muslin strip in half crosswise to find the center. Lightly crease the fold.
- Center a red F on the fold, 1 1/4" from the edge. Pin it in place.
- Referring to the quilt photo, lay the remaining red F's on the strip, evenly spacing them and keeping them 1 1/4" from the long sides of the muslin strip and approximately 3 1/2" from the ends. Pin them in place.
- Place 4 1/2" green strips between the flowers and pin them in place.
- Place the leaves on each side of the strip and pin them in place.
- Lifting one piece at a time, lightly make a pencil mark on the muslin strip to indicate placement of the appliqué pieces. Remove the pins.
- Appliqué the pieces to the muslin strip in the following order:
  4 1/2" green stems
  Red F's
  Green D's
  Yellow G's
- Trim the appliquéd strip to 8 1/2" wide to complete the center section, keeping the design centered on the strip.
- Measure the length of a block row. If necessary, trim the center section to that measurement.

ASSEMBLY
- Sew the appliquéd center section between the rows.
- Sew a 3 1/2" x 77" muslin strip between a 2 1/2" x 77" red strip and a 4 1/2" x 77" green strip to make a short border. Make 2.
- Sew a 3 1/2" x 91" muslin strip between a 2 1/2" x 91" red strip and a 4 1/2" x 91" green strip to make a long border. Make 2.
- Center and sew the short borders to the short sides of the quilt. Start and stop stitching 1/4" from each edge and backstitch.
- In the same manner, sew the long borders to the long sides of the quilt.
- Miter the corners as described in the *General Directions*.
- Finish the quilt as described in the *General Directions*. Use the 2 1/2" x 90" red strips for the binding.

Star Within a Star

Piece no-template stars—the scrappier the better!

QUILT SIZE: 78" x 95"
BLOCK SIZE: 10 1/2" square

MATERIALS
Yardage is estimated for 44" fabric.
- Assorted scraps of light, medium and dark prints totaling at least 6 yards
- 3 1/4 yards muslin
- 3/4 yard dark print for the binding
- 5 3/4 yards backing fabric
- 82" x 99" piece of batting

CUTTING
Dimensions include a 1/4" seam allowance. Cut lengthwise strips before cutting other pieces from the same yardage.

For each of 48 blocks:
NOTE: *You will use 3 prints in each of the 48 blocks. Group the pieces for each block as you cut them.*
- Cut 1: 3" square, first print
- Cut 8: 1 3/4" squares, first print
- Cut 4: 3 3/8" squares, second print, then cut them in half diagonally to yield 8 triangles
- Cut 4: 4" squares, third print
- Cut 1: 4 3/4" square, third print, then cut it in quarters diagonally to yield 4 triangles

Also:
- Cut 2: 4 1/2" x 94 1/2" strips, muslin
- Cut 1: 3 1/2" x 77 1/2" strip, muslin
- Cut 2: 3 1/2" x 74" strips, muslin
- Cut 2: 3 1/2" x 69 1/2" strips, muslin
- Cut 1: 4 1/2" x 69 1/2" strip, muslin
- Cut 2: 3 1/2" x 11" strips, muslin
- Cut 192: 1 3/4" squares, muslin
- Cut 192: 1 3/4" x 3" rectangles, muslin
- Cut 9: 2 1/2" x 44" strips, binding fabric

PIECING
For each block:
- Draw a diagonal line from corner to corner on the wrong side of each 1 3/4"

Connie Egli of Riverside, Pennsylvania, stitched **"Star Within a Star"** (78" x 95") using contrasting prints from her scrapbag. She used muslin to unify the blocks and frame the center section.

first print square.
- Lay a marked 1 3/4" first print square on a 1 3/4" x 3" muslin rectangle, aligning the outer edes, as shown. Sew on the drawn line.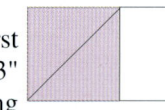
- Press the print square toward the corner and trim the seam allowance to 1/4".
- Lay a marked 1 3/4" first print square on the opposite end of the muslin rectangle, as shown. Sew on the drawn line. Press and trim, as before. Make 4.

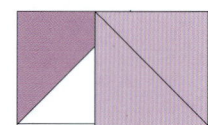

- Lay out the 4 pieced units, the matching 3" print square and four 1 3/4" muslin squares, as shown.

- Stitch the units into rows and join the rows to make a Center Star.
- Sew 2 second print triangles to a 4" third print square to make a corner unit. Make 4.
- Sew third print triangles to 2 of the corner units.

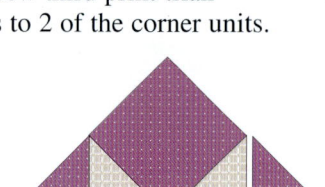

- Lay out the Center Star and the pieced units, as shown. Join them to complete a Star Within a Star block. Make 48.

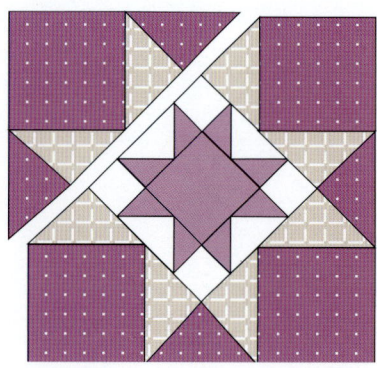

- Referring to the quilt photo, lay out the blocks in a pleasing color arrangement. You'll assemble the quilt top in sections.
- Sew blocks for the center section into 7 rows of 4.
- Sew 7 blocks in a row to make a side section. Make 2.
- Join 6 blocks and two 3 1/2" x 11" muslin strips to make the bottom section. Set it aside.

- Sew the 3 1/2" x 74" muslin strips to the long sides of the center section.
- Sew the side sections to the long sides of the quilt.
- Sew the 3 1/2" x 69 1/2" muslin strips to the short sides of the quilt.
- Sew the bottom section to one short side of the quilt.
- Sew the 4 1/2" x 69 1/2" muslin strip to the bottom of the quilt.
- Sew the 4 1/2" x 94 1/2" muslin strips to the sides of the quilt.
- Finish the quilt as described in the *General Directions,* using the 2 1/2" x 44" strips for the binding.

Posies

Old-fashioned blossoms from Grandmother's Flower Garden.

QUILT SIZE: 77 1/4" x 95 3/4"
BLOCK SIZE: 11" square

MATERIALS
Yardage is estimated for 44" fabric.
- 3 5/8 yards muslin
- 1/4 yard red print for the flower centers
- Assorted print scraps totaling at least 1 3/4 yards for the flowers and binding
- 3/8 yard medium green print for the stems
- 1/2 yard dark green print for the leaves
- 3 yards small-scale brown print for the sashing
- 1 1/2 yards medium-scale brown print for the setting and corner triangles
- 5 3/4 yards backing fabric
- 81" x 100" piece of batting

CUTTING
The leaf appliqué piece on page 18 is full size and does not include a seam allowance. Mark the leaves on the right side of the fabric and add a 3/16" to 1/4" turn-under allowance when cutting them out. The A piece is full size and includes a 1/4" seam allowance, as do all dimensions given. Cut the lengthwise brown print strips before cutting other pieces from the same yardage.

- Cut 32: 11 1/2" squares, muslin
- Cut 32: A, red print, for the flower centers
- Cut 38: 2 1/2" x 12" strips, assorted prints, for the binding
- Cut 192: A's in 32 matching sets of 6, assorted prints
- Cut 32: 1 1/2" x 7" strips, medium green print, for the stems
- Cut 64: leaves, dark green print
- Cut 1: 2 1/2" x 104 1/2" lengthwise strip, small-scale brown print
- Cut 2: 2 1/2" x 93 1/2" lengthwise strips, small-scale brown print
- Cut 2: 2 1/2" x 67 1/2" lengthwise

Margot Cohen of Cedarhurst, New York, used a charming assortment of reproduction fabrics in her quaint ***Posies*** quilt (77 1/4" x 95 3/4"). Sashing between the blocks gives the impression of an old-fashioned flower garden seen through lattice.

Full-Size Pattern and Appliqué Pieces for Posies

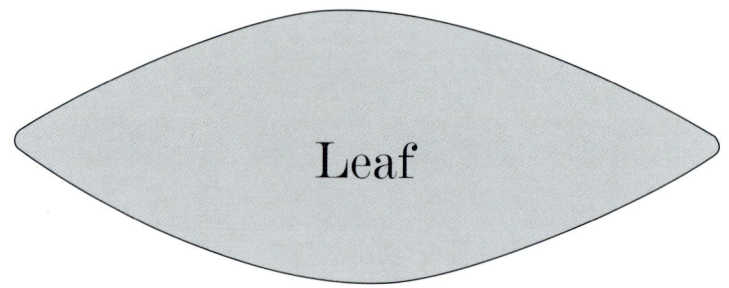

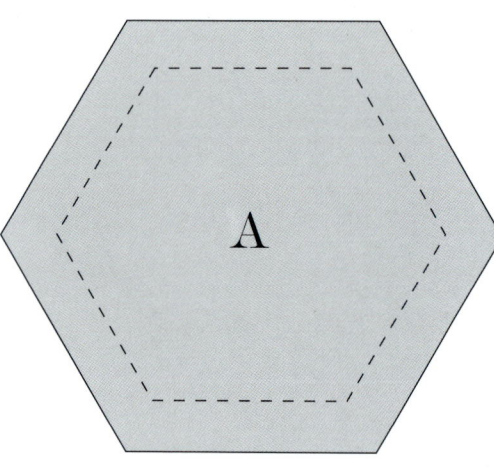

strips, small-scale brown print
• Cut 2: 2 1/2" x 41 1/2" lengthwise strips, small-scale brown print
• Cut 2: 2 1/2" x 15 1/2" sashing strips, small-scale brown print
• Cut 40: 2 1/2" x 11 1/2" sashing strips, small-scale brown print
• Cut 4: 19 5/8" squares, medium-scale brown print, then cut them in quarters diagonally to yield 16 setting triangles. You will use 14.
• Cut 2: 11 1/2" squares, medium-scale brown print, then cut them in half diagonally to yield 4 corner triangles

PIECING
• Take one red A and 6 matching print A's. Place the red print A and one print A right sides together. Join them by stitching along one side, beginning, ending and backstitching at the 1/4" seamlines.
• In the same manner, sew another A to an adjacent side of the red A. Then sew the seam between the 2 matching A's.
• Continue adding A's until you have completed a flower. Make 32.

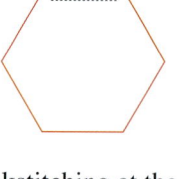

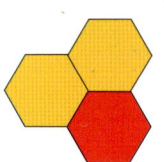

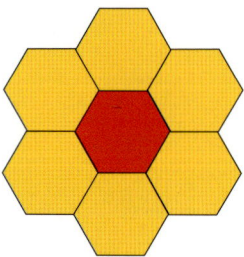

APPLIQUÉ
• Fold a 1 1/2" x 7" medium green print strip in half lengthwise, right side out. Using a 1/4" seam allowance, sew along the long raw edge. Trim the seam allowance to about 3/16". Then roll the seam to the center of the strip and press it open. You'll have a 1/2"-wide stem ready to appliqué. Prepare the remaining 1 1/2" x 7" medium green print strips in the same manner.

• Place an 11 1/2" muslin square on point, on a flat work surface. Position a stem with the lower end at the bottom corner of the square, covering the raw edges of the corner. Appliqué the stem to the square.

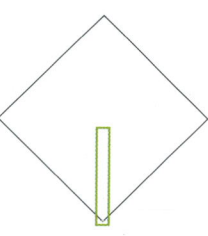

• Place a flower on the square so that it covers the top end of the stem. Appliqué it in place. Appliqué a leaf on each side of the stem to complete the block. Trim the bottom edge of the stem even with the block. Make 32.

• Place the blocks right side down, on a padded surface such as a clean terry cloth towel. Press.

ASSEMBLY
NOTE: *Refer to the Assembly Diagram for the following steps.*
• Lay out 20 of the blocks on point in 5 horizontal rows of 4. Leave some space between blocks for the sashing. Place the remaining 12 blocks in the spaces between the rows of 4.
• Place 2 1/2" x 11 1/2" brown print sashing strips between the blocks and at the ends of each diagonal row.
• Sew the blocks and sashing strips into diagonal rows.
• Sew 2 1/2" x 15 1/2" brown print sashing strips to the outer edge of the upper left block and the lower right block.
• Place the remaining sashing strips between the appropriate length rows. Sew the rows and sashing strips into diagonal rows.
• Sew brown print setting triangles to the ends of the diagonal rows.
• Sew a brown print corner triangle to each corner of the quilt.
• Sew the 2 1/2" x 12" print strips together with diagonal seams, to make a pieced strip.
• Finish the quilt as described in the *General Directions,* using the pieced strip for the binding.

Assembly Diagram

Magnolia

Grow a beautiful garden with soft pastel prints.

QUILT SIZE: 95" x 117"
BLOCK SIZE: 8" square

MATERIALS
Yardage is estimated for 44" fabric.
- Assorted pastel prints in peach, pink, yellow, purple and blue, totaling at least 2 yards
- 2 yards green
- 6 yards white
- 8 1/2 yards backing fabric
- 99" x 121" piece of batting

CUTTING
The pattern piece on page 20 is full size and includes a 1/4" seam allowance, as do all dimensions given. Cut the lengthwise white strips before cutting smaller pieces from that fabric.

For each of 72 blocks:
- Cut 1: A, pastel print
- Cut 1: AR, same print

Also:
- Cut 72: 1 1/2" squares, assorted prints
- Cut 72: 4 1/2" squares, assorted prints
- Cut 2 1/2"-wide bias strips, green, to create a strip approximately 500" long when joined, for the binding
- Cut 72: A, green
- Cut 72: AR, green
- Cut 6: 10 1/2" x 100" lengthwise strips, white
- Cut 3: 2 1/2" x 100" lengthwise strips, white
- Cut 144: A, white
- Cut 144: AR, white
- Cut 216: 2 1/2" squares, white
- Cut 216: 1 1/2" squares, white

PIECING
- Sew three 1 1/2" white squares and one 1 1/2" print square together, as shown, to form a Four Patch.

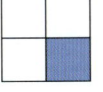

Eva M. Ross of Wichita, Kansas, had fun selecting fabrics from her extensive stash to make the prizewinning **"Magnolia"** *(95" x 117").*

- Sew a white A to a green A along their long sides to form a pieced rectangle.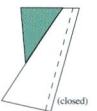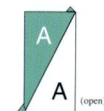
- In the same manner, sew a green AR to a white AR.
- In the same manner, sew a pastel print A to a white A and a same print AR to a white AR.
- Lay out the four pieced rectangles, the Four Patch, three 2 1/2" white squares and a 4 1/2" print square, as shown.
- Sew the units into rows and join the rows to complete a block. Make 72.

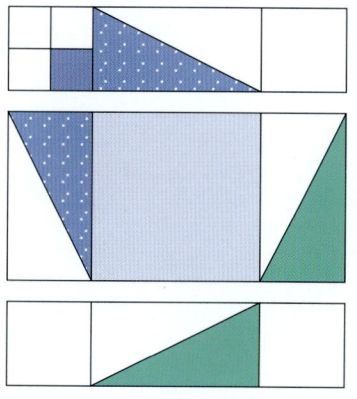

- Referring to the quilt photo as needed, lay out the blocks in 6 vertical rows of 12, alternating the direction of each flower.

Sew the blocks into rows.
- Measure the length of the rows. Trim the 2 1/2" x 100" white strips and four 10 1/2" x 100" white strips to that measurement.
- Sew a 2 1/2"-wide white strip between 2 rows of blocks to form a vertical pieced strip. Make 3.
- Lay out the 3 vertical pieced strips, placing 10 1/2"-wide white strips between them and along the outer long edges of the quilt. Join the strips.
- Measure the width of the quilt. Trim the remaining 10 1/2" x 100" white strips to that measurement and sew them to the top and bottom of the quilt.
- Finish the quilt as described in the *General Directions*. After it is quilted, mark evenly spaced arcs along the outer edges of the quilt. Trim the edges along the marked line. Use the 2 1/2"-wide green bias strip for the binding.

Full-Size Pattern Piece for Magnolia

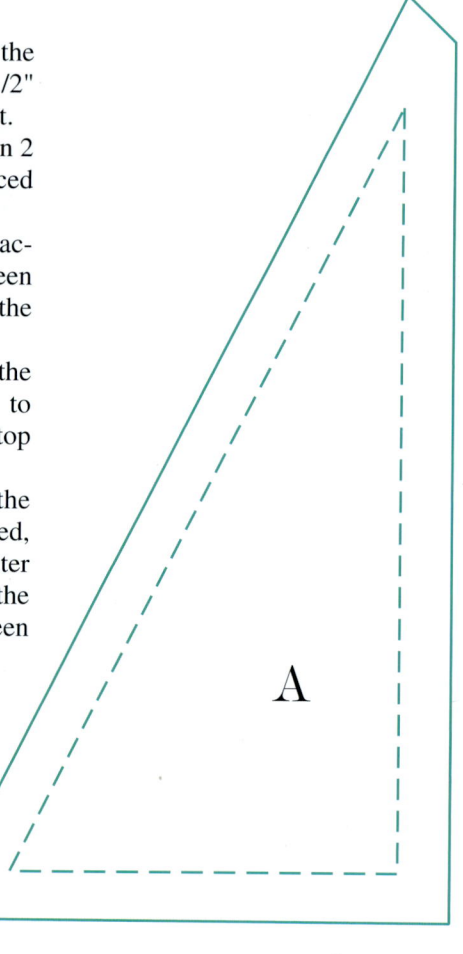

Plaid Stars, Rolling Stars

A time-honored pattern gets a bright new lease on life.

QUILT SIZE: 80" x 103 1/2"
BLOCK SIZES:
Rolling Star: 11 1/2" square
Lemoyne Star: 5 1/8" square

MATERIALS
Yardage is estimated for 44" fabric.
- 2 3/4 yards blue paisley for the Rolling Star blocks, sashing and outer border
- 1 yard navy print for the Rolling Star blocks and sashing
- 3 yards cream print for the sashing, Lemoyne Star blocks and inner border
- 1/2 yard light tan print
- 1/2 yard tan print
- 1/2 yard burgundy print
- 1/2 yard rose print
- 1/2 yard brown print
- Assorted prints for the Lemoyne Star blocks and the pieced border totaling 1 1/4 yards
- 1 yard dark tan print for the pieced border
- 7/8 yard navy print for the binding
- 6 1/4 yards of backing fabric
- 84" x 108" piece of batting

CUTTING
Pattern pieces on page 22 are full size and include a 1/4" seam allowance as do all dimensions given. We recommend making a sample block before cutting fabric for the entire quilt. Label each group of pieces as you cut them.

For the Rolling Star blocks and half-blocks:
- Cut 44: A, blue paisley
- Cut 44: A, navy print
- Cut 44: 2 7/8" squares, light tan print
- Cut 38: 2 7/8" squares, tan print

- Cut 3: 4 5/8" squares, tan print, then cut them in quarters diagonally to yield 12 triangles
- Cut 44: A, burgundy print
- Cut 44: A, rose print
- Cut 19: 4 1/4" squares, brown print, then cut them in half diagonally to yield 38 large triangles
- Cut 3: 4 5/8" squares, brown print, then cut them in quarters diagonally to yield 12 small triangles

For the Lemoyne Star blocks:
- Cut 28: B, dark prints, in 7 sets of 4 matching pieces
- Cut 28: B, medium prints, in 7 sets of 4 matching pieces
- Cut 28: 2" squares, cream print
- Cut 7: 3 3/8" squares, cream print, then cut them in quarters diagonally to yield 28 triangles. Label them A.

For the Lemoyne Star half-blocks:
- Cut 20: B, dark prints, in 10 sets of 2 matching pieces
- Cut 20: B, medium prints, in 10 sets of 2 matching pieces
- Cut 10: 2" squares, cream print
- Cut 10: 3 3/8" squares, cream print, then cut them in quarters diagonally to yield 40 triangles. Label them A.

For the Corner blocks:
- Cut 4: A, blue paisley
- Cut 4: A, navy print
- Cut 4: A, burgundy print
- Cut 4: A, rose print
- Cut 4: 2 7/8" squares, cream print
- Cut 4: 3 1/4" squares, cream print, then cut them in half diagonally to yield 8 triangles. Label them B.
- Cut 2: 4 5/8" squares, cream print, then cut them in quarters diagonally to yield 8 triangles. Label them C.

For the Pieced border:
- Cut 39: 5 1/4" squares, assorted medium and dark prints, then cut them in quarters diagonally to yield 156 large triangles
- Cut 2: 2 7/8" squares, medium and dark prints, then cut them in half diagonally to yield 4 small triangles
- Cut 18: 5 1/4" squares, dark tan print, then cut them in quarters diagonally to yield 72 triangles
- Cut 17: 5 1/4" squares, cream print, then cut them in quarters diagonally to yield 68 triangles. Label them D.
- Cut 6: 2 7/8" squares, cream print, then cut them in half diagonally to yield 12 triangles. Label them E.

Also:
- Cut 2: 5" x 94" strips, blue paisley, for the outer border

Sharyn Craig based her **"Plaid Stars, Rolling Stars"** quilt (80" x 103 1/2") on the old-fashioned Rolling Star block. Using it as her creative springboard, Sharyn placed the blocks on point and added pieced sashing with LeMoyne Stars at the intersections. A Streak o' Lightning border provides an energetic finishing touch.

- Cut 2: 5" x 79 1/2" strips, blue paisley, for the outer border
- Cut 24: 1 3/4" x 12" strips, blue paisley
- Cut 24: 1 3/4" x 12" strips, navy print
- Cut 24: 3 1/8" x 12" strips, cream print
- Cut 2: 7" x 71" strips, cream print
- Cut 2: 7" x 60 1/2" strips, cream print
- Cut 8: 1 1/2" x 44" strips, dark tan print
- Cut 10: 2 1/2" x 44" strips, navy print, for the binding

PIECING
For each Rolling Star block:
- Place a navy print A on a blue paisley A, right sides together. Sew to the 1/4" seamline and backstitch. Make 4
- Set a 2 7/8" light tan print square into each unit, as shown. Make 4.
- Sew the 4 units together, matching the center seams, to make a Star unit, as shown, stopping and backstitching 1/4" from each edge.

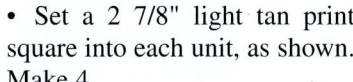

- Set 2 7/8" tan print squares into the Star unit stopping and backstitching at each outside edge.
- Turn the Star unit, placing the tan print squares at the top, bottom and sides.

- Set a burgundy A into the top right position of the Star unit and a rose print A into the top left position, as shown.
- Repeat, sewing burgundy and rose print A's to the remaining sides of the Star unit.
- Sew large brown print triangles to each corner to complete a block. Make 8.

For each Rolling Star half-block:

- Join a navy print A and a blue paisley A and set a 2 7/8" light tan print square into the unit, as before. Make 2. Join them to make a half-star unit.
- Set a 2 7/8" tan print square into the half-star unit. Sew tan print triangles to opposite sides, as shown.

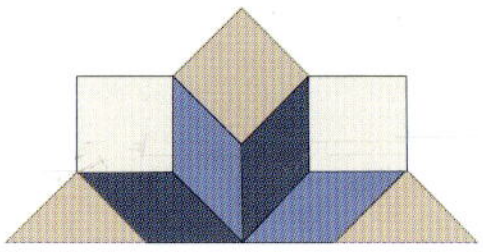

- Sew a burgundy print A into the top, right side of the unit and a rose print A into the top, left side, as before.
- Set a burgundy print A into the left side and a rose print A into the right side. Sew a large brown print triangle to the top of the unit and 2 small brown print triangles to the sides to complete a Rolling Star half-block. Make 6. Set them aside.

For each Lemoyne Star block:

- Sew a dark print B and a medium print B together and set a 2" cream print square into the unit, as before. Make 4.

- Sew the 4 units together, matching the center seams, to make a Star unit.
- Set 4 cream print triangle A's into the Star unit to complete a block. Make 7.

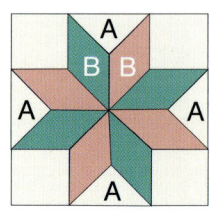

For each Lemoyne Star half-block:

- Sew a dark print B to a medium print B, as before. Set a cream print triangle A into the unit, as shown. Make 2.

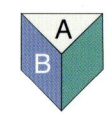

- Sew the units together to make a half-star unit.
- Set a 2" cream print square into the half-star unit. Sew cream print triangle A's to opposite sides of the unit, as shown. Make 10. Set them aside.

For each Corner block:

- Sew a rose print A to a navy print A, as before. Set a cream print triangle C into the unit.
- In the same manner, sew a blue paisley A to a burgundy print A and set a cream print triangle C into the unit.
- Join the units to make a half-star unit, keeping the rose print A toward the left. Set a 2 7/8" cream print square into the half-star unit. Sew cream print triangle B's to opposite sides to complete a Corner block. Make 4.

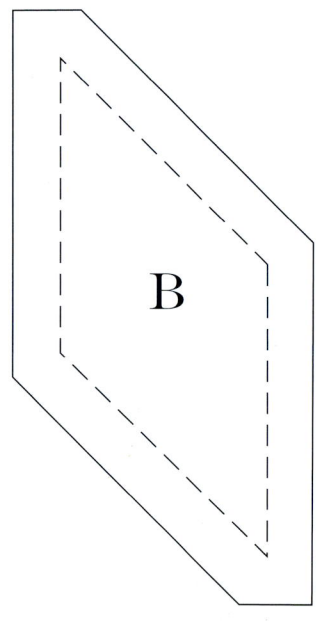

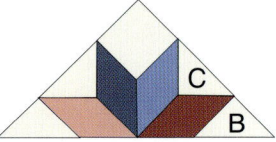

For the sashing:

- Sew a 1 3/4" x 12" navy print strip to a 3 1/8" x 12" cream print strip, right sides together along their length. Sew a 1 3/4" x 12" navy print strip to the opposite side of the cream print strip to make a pieced sashing strip. Make 12.
- In the same manner, make 12 sashing strips using the 1 3/4" x 12" blue paisley strips and the remaining 3 1/8" x 12" cream print strips.

ASSEMBLY

- Referring to the quilt photo on page 21, lay out the Rolling Star blocks and half-blocks, the Lemoyne Star blocks and half-blocks, the Corner units and the pieced sashing strips.
- Sew the blocks, half-blocks and pieced sashing strips into diagonal rows and join the rows. Sew the corner units to the corners.
- Sew the 7" x 71" cream print strips to the long sides of the quilt.
- Sew the 7" x 60 1/2" cream print strips to the short sides of the quilt. Set it aside.

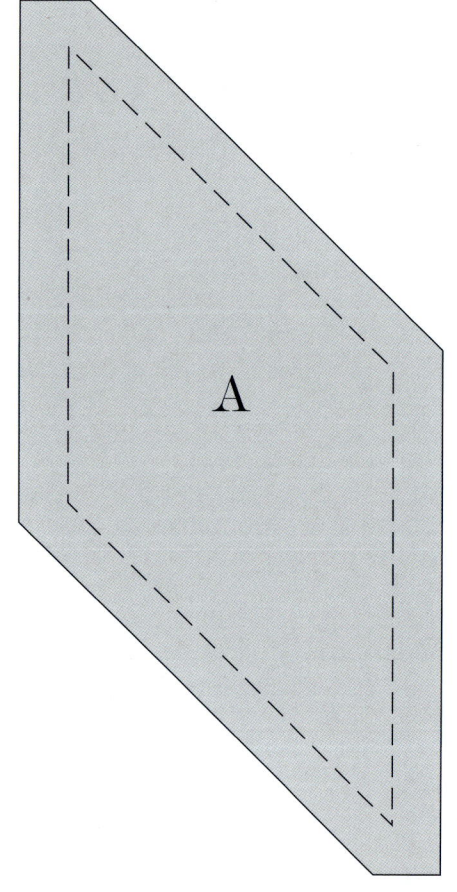

For the pieced border:
- Sew 21 large assorted print triangles and 20 cream print triangle D's into a row. Sew a cream print triangle E to each end to complete a long pieced border, as shown. Make 2.
- In the same manner, join 15 large

assorted print triangles, 14 cream print triangle D's and 2 cream print triangle E's to make a short pieced border. Make 2.
- Sew a small print triangle and a cream print triangle E together to make a pieced square. Make 4.
- Sew a pieced square to each end of the short pieced borders, placing the cream print triangles together.
- Sew the long pieced borders to the long sides of the quilt, placing the cream print triangles against the quilt.
- Sew the short pieced borders to the short sides of the quilt in the same manner.
- Sew 22 large assorted print triangles and 21 dark tan print triangles into a row to make a long pieced border. Make 2.
- In the same manner, join 16 large assorted print triangles and 15 dark tan print triangles to make a short pieced border. Make 2.
- Sew the long pieced borders to the long sides of the quilt, placing the dark print triangles against the quilt.
- Sew the short pieced borders to the short sides of the quilt in the same manner.
- Sew 2 large dark print triangles together to make a corner triangle. Make 4.
- Sew the corner triangles to the corners of the quilt.
- Sew the 1 1/2" x 44" dark tan print strips together, end to end, to make a pieced strip.
- Cut two 92" lengths from the pieced strip. Sew them to the long sides of the quilt.
- Cut two 70 1/2" lengths from the pieced strip. Sew them to the short sides of the quilt.
- Sew the 5" x 94" blue paisley strips to the long sides of the quilt.
- Sew the 5" x 79 1/2" blue paisley strips to the short sides of the quilt.
- Finish the quilt as described in the *General Directions,* using the 2 1/2" x 44" navy print strips for the binding.

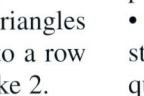

Postage Stamp Basket

This traditional block inspired a commemorative Folk Art stamp.

Shown on page 24
QUILT SIZE: 73" x 90 1/2"
BLOCK SIZE: 15" square

MATERIALS
Yardage is estimated for 44" fabric.
- Assorted scraps of light, medium and dark prints totaling 2 1/2 yards
- 3 1/4 yards muslin
- 2 5/8 yards red print
- 5 1/2 yards backing fabric
- 77" x 95" piece of batting

CUTTING
Appliqué pattern A on page 24 is full size and does not include a 1/4" seam allowance on the curved edges. Make a template of the pattern piece and cut it out. Trace around the template on the right side of the fabric and add a 1/8" to 3/16" turn-under allowance to the curved edges when cutting the pieces out. All other dimensions include a 1/4" seam allowance.

For each of 80 Baskets:
- Cut 1: A, print
- Cut 1: 5 7/8" square, same print, then cut it in half diagonally to yield 2 large triangles
NOTE: *You will use one large triangle for each Basket. Keep the other one for another basket.*
- Cut 1: 3 3/8" square, same print, then cut it in half diagonally to yield 2 small triangles

Also:
- Cut 80: 5 7/8" squares, muslin, then cut them in half diagonally
- Cut 160: 3" squares, muslin
- Cut 16: 3" x 15 1/2" strips, red print, for the sashing
- Cut 5: 3" x 88" strips, red print, for the sashing and outer border
- Cut 2: 3" x 75" strips, red print, for the outer border
- Cut 5: 2 1/2" x 72" strips, red print, for the binding

PIECING
- Center a print A on a muslin triangle, aligning the straight edges of the A with the edge of the muslin triangle, as shown. Pin them together.

- Use the tip of your needle to turn under the seam allowance as you appliqué the print A to the muslin triangle.
- Sew a matching large print triangle to the appliquéd unit to make a basket unit. Set it aside.
- Sew a matching small print triangle to a 3" muslin square to make a side unit. Make another

side unit, reversing the direction of the small print triangle, as shown on page 24.

Postage Stamp Basket

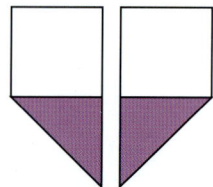

- Sew the side units to the Basket unit. Stitch a muslin triangle to the bottom to make a Basket. Make 80.

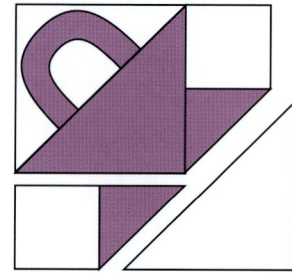

- Lay out 4 Baskets and join them to make a Postage Stamp Basket block. Make 20.

"Postage Stamp Basket" *(73" x 90 1/2") is a traditional pattern that combines appliqué and piecing. Ruby Moss, of Fairfield, California, hand pieced each basket from a different print and used red calico for the sashing.*

- Lay out 5 blocks and four 3" x 15 1/2" red print strips. Join them to make a vertical row. Make 4.
- Measure the length of one vertical row and trim the 3" x 88" red print strips to that measurement.
- Referring to the quilt photo, sew trimmed strips between the rows and one on each side.
- Measure the width of the quilt. Trim the 3" x 75" red print strips to that measurement and sew them to the remaining sides of the quilt.
- Finish the quilt as described in the *General Directions*. Use the 2 1/2" x 72" red print strips for the binding.

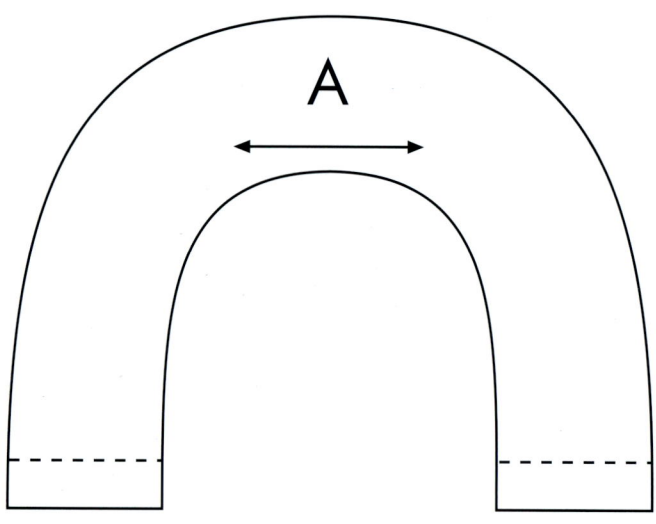

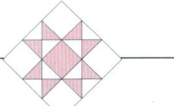

Bluebird of Happiness

Let your creativity bloom!

*Debbie Ballard's summery medallion quilt **"Bluebird of Happiness"** (84 1/2" square) evokes the naive charm of 19th century folk art. Pieced borders provide an appropriate geometric counterpoint to the primitive appliqué motifs. Quilted by Elsie Vredenburg.*

Bluebird of Happiness

QUILT SIZE: 84 1/2" square
OHIO STAR BLOCK: 9 3/4" square

NOTE: *These directions will give your quilt a slightly different look. All 4 Ohio Star borders will be constructed to look like the side borders in the quilt shown.*

MATERIALS

Yardage is estimated for 44" fabric.

- Red solid and assorted red prints totaling 1 yard
- 6 yards white
- 1 1/4 yards dark green for the stems and leaves
- 10" square of dark blue print for the vase
- 5" x 7" piece of medium blue for the bird
- Assorted print scraps for the appliquéd flowers
- 24 prints each at least 9" square for the Ohio Star blocks
- 2 yards dark blue for the third border and the binding
- 7 1/2 yards backing fabric
- 89" square of batting

CUTTING

Appliqué pieces on pages 27-31 are full size and do not include a seam allowance. Make templates for each of the pattern pieces and cut them out. Trace around the templates on the right side of the fabric and add a 3/16" turn-under allowance when cutting the pieces out. Pattern piece A includes a 1/4" seam allowance as do all dimensions given. Cut lengthwise strips before cutting other pieces from the same yardage.

- Cut 2: 1 1/4" x 33 3/4" strips, red solid
- Cut 25: A, red solid and assorted red prints
- Cut 11: AR, red solid and prints
- Cut 2: 9 1/8" x 60 1/2" lengthwise strips, white
- Cut 2: 8 1/2" x 43 1/4" lengthwise strips, white
- Cut 8: 3 1/4" x 10 1/4" lengthwise strips, white
- Cut 2: 1 1/8" x 33 3/4" strips, white
- Cut 1: 33 3/4" square, white
- Cut 25: A, white
- Cut 11: AR, white
- Cut 48: 4 1/2" squares, white
- Cut 96: 3 3/4" squares, white
- Cut 12: 1" x 38" bias strips, dark green
- Cut 1: 1 1/2" x 18" bias strip, dark green
- Cut 2: 2 1/2" x 64 1/2" lengthwise strips, dark blue, for the third border
- Cut 2: 2 1/2" x 60 1/2" lengthwise strips, dark blue, for the third border
- Cut 6: 2 1/2" x 64" strips dark blue, for the binding

For each of 24 Ohio Star blocks:
- Cut 2: 4 1/2" squares, one print
- Cut 1: 3 3/4" square, same print

For the Appliqué:
NOTE: *Each flower in this quilt is unique. We have provided flower patterns but feel free to draw your own flowers as you wish. All of the flower patterns we've provided are labeled F. All of the leaf patterns are labeled L. All of the flower and leaf patterns that are used in the center medallion are numbered to correspond with the placement diagram. Refer to the quilt photo when cutting the appliqué pieces.*

- Cut flowers of assorted colors
- Cut leaves, green
- Cut 1: bird, medium blue
- Cut 1: vase, dark blue print

PREPARATION

- Join the 1"-wide dark green bias strips with diagonal seams to make a long pieced strip.
- Fold the pieced bias strip in half lengthwise, right side out. Sew 1/4" from the raw edge.
- Press the strip, centering the stitching line, as shown.
- Refold the strip the way it was for stitching. Carefully trim the seam allowance away just inside the stitching line. You now have a 1/4"-wide bias strip prepared for appliqué.
- Repeat for the 1 1/2"-wide dark green bias strip to yield a 1/2"-wide strip to use for the stem of the F-7 flower.

DIRECTIONS

- Lay out the 33 3/4" square of white fabric. Using the quilt photo and the numbered Placement Diagram on page 27 as guides, position the vase, bird and flowers properly. Use pieces of the 1/4"-wide green bias strip for stems. Use the 1/2"-wide bias strip for the stem of flower F-7. Pin the pieces in place. Appliqué the pieces to the white square, starting with the vase. Leave the top edge unstitched then stitch the stems, leaves, flowers and centers as shown in the placement diagram. Appliqué the top edge of the vase after the stems have been stitched.

- Sew a red A to a white A to make a border unit, as shown. Press the seam allowances toward the red. Make 25.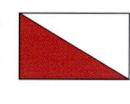

- Lay out 7 border units. Sew them together to make a pieced border, as shown. Make 2.

- Stitch a 1 1/4" x 33 3/4" red strip to a 1 1/8" x 33 3/4" white strip to make a pieced strip. Make 2.
- Sew a pieced strip to a pieced border, keeping the white strip against the white triangles. Make 2.

- Sew these borders to the sides of the quilt center, keeping the red triangles against the quilt center. Refer to the quilt photo, as necessary.
- Join the remaining 11 border units to make a pieced border, as shown. Sew the pieced border to the bottom of the quilt, keeping the red triangles against the quilt.

- Stitch a white AR to a red AR to make a reverse border unit, as shown. Make 11.
- Join the reverse border units to make a pieced border, as shown.

- Sew the pieced border to the top of the quilt, keeping the red triangles against the quilt. Set it aside.

For the appliquéd border:
- Referring to the quilt photo for the vertical appliquéd borders, lay the 1/2"-wide green bias strip like a meandering vine on an 8 1/2" x 43 1/4" white strip. Carefully pin the vine in place. When you are satisfied with the position, baste it in place. Trim the ends of the vine even with the raw edge of the white strip.
- Place flowers along the vine, keeping them at least 1/2" from the edges of the white strip. Pin the flowers, stems, and leaves in place, tucking the stems under the edge of the vine. Appliqué the stems first, then the vine. Appliqué the leaves,

flowers and flower centers.
• Repeat for the remaining 8 1/2" x 43 1/4" white vertical appliquéd border strip and the 9 1/8" x 60 1/2" white horizontal appliquéd border strips.
• Pin, then stitch the vertical border strips to the sides of the quilt.
• Pin, then stitch the horizontal border strips to the top and bottom of the quilt.
• Stitch the 2 1/2" x 60 1/2" dark blue strips to the sides of the quilt.
• Stitch the 2 1/2" x 64 1/2" dark blue strips to the top and bottom of the quilt. Set it aside.

For the Ohio Star blocks:
• Draw 2 diagonal lines from corner to corner on the wrong side of each 4 1/2" white square.

For each star:
• Place a marked white square on a 4 1/2" print square, right sides together. Sew 1/4" away on both sides of one diagonal line, as shown. Make 2.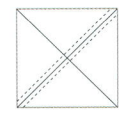
• Cut the squares on the diagonal lines to yield 8 pieced triangles.
• Join 2 pieced triangles to make a pieced square, as shown. Make 4.
• Lay out the pieced squares, a matching 3 3/4" print square and four 3 3/4" white squares in 3 rows of 3. Stitch the squares into rows, then join the rows to complete an Ohio Star block. Make 30.

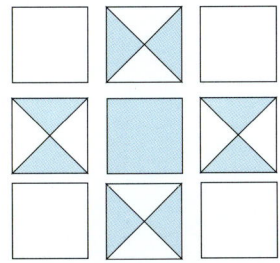

• Join 6 Ohio Star blocks to make a row. Stitch a 3 1/4" x 10 1/4" white strip to each end of the row, as shown, to make a Star border. Make 4.

• Stitch 2 Star borders to the sides of the quilt.
• Stitch an Ohio Star block to each end of the remaining Star borders.
• Stitch these Star borders to the top and bottom of the quilt.
• Finish the quilt according to the *General Directions,* using the 2 1/2" x 64" dark blue strips for the binding.

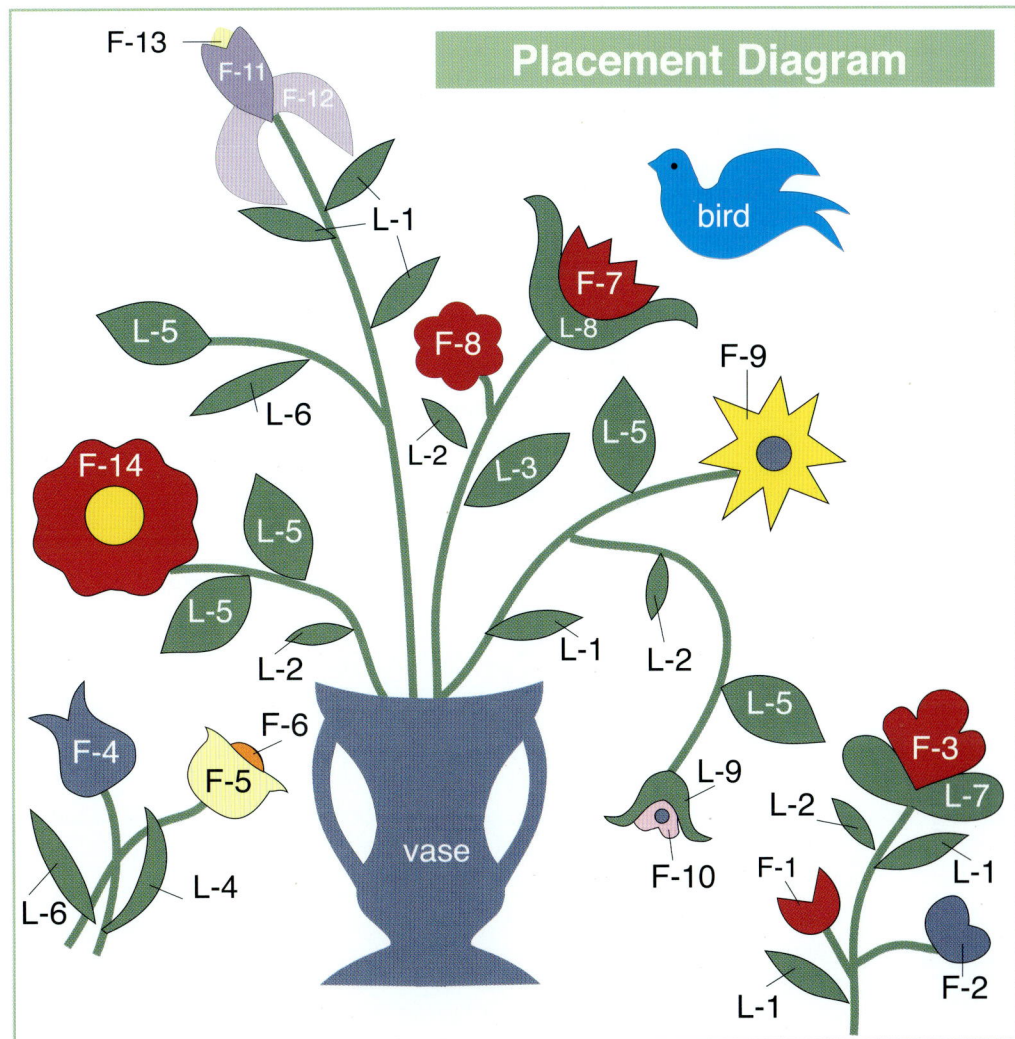

Placement Diagram

Full-size Appliqué Pieces for Bluebird of Happiness continued on pages 28 - 31

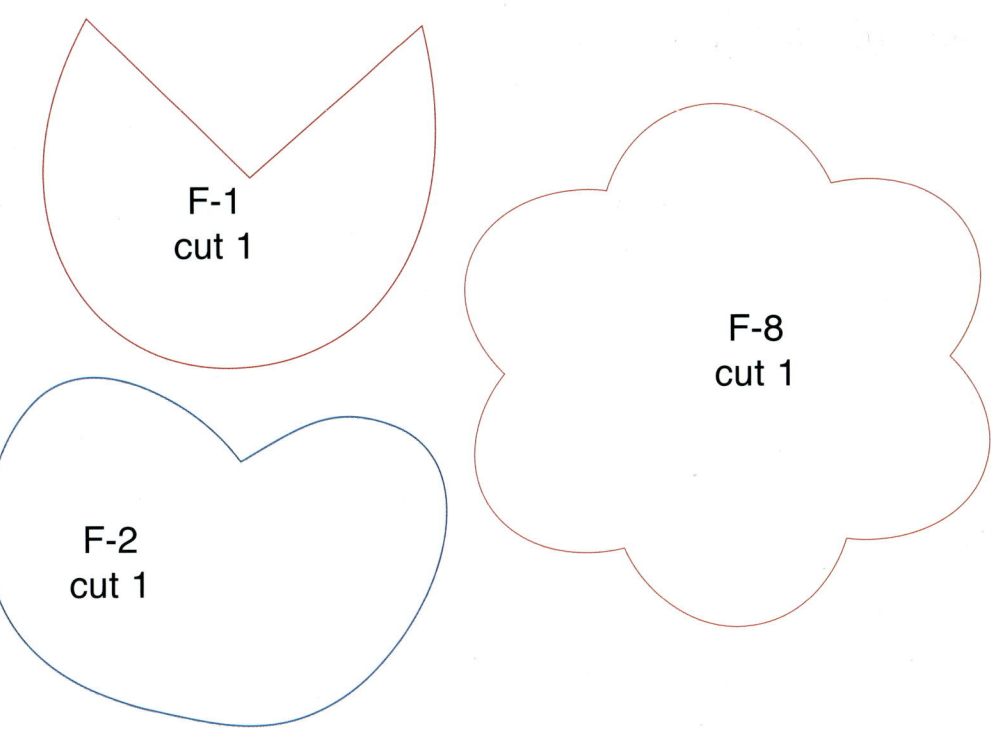

27

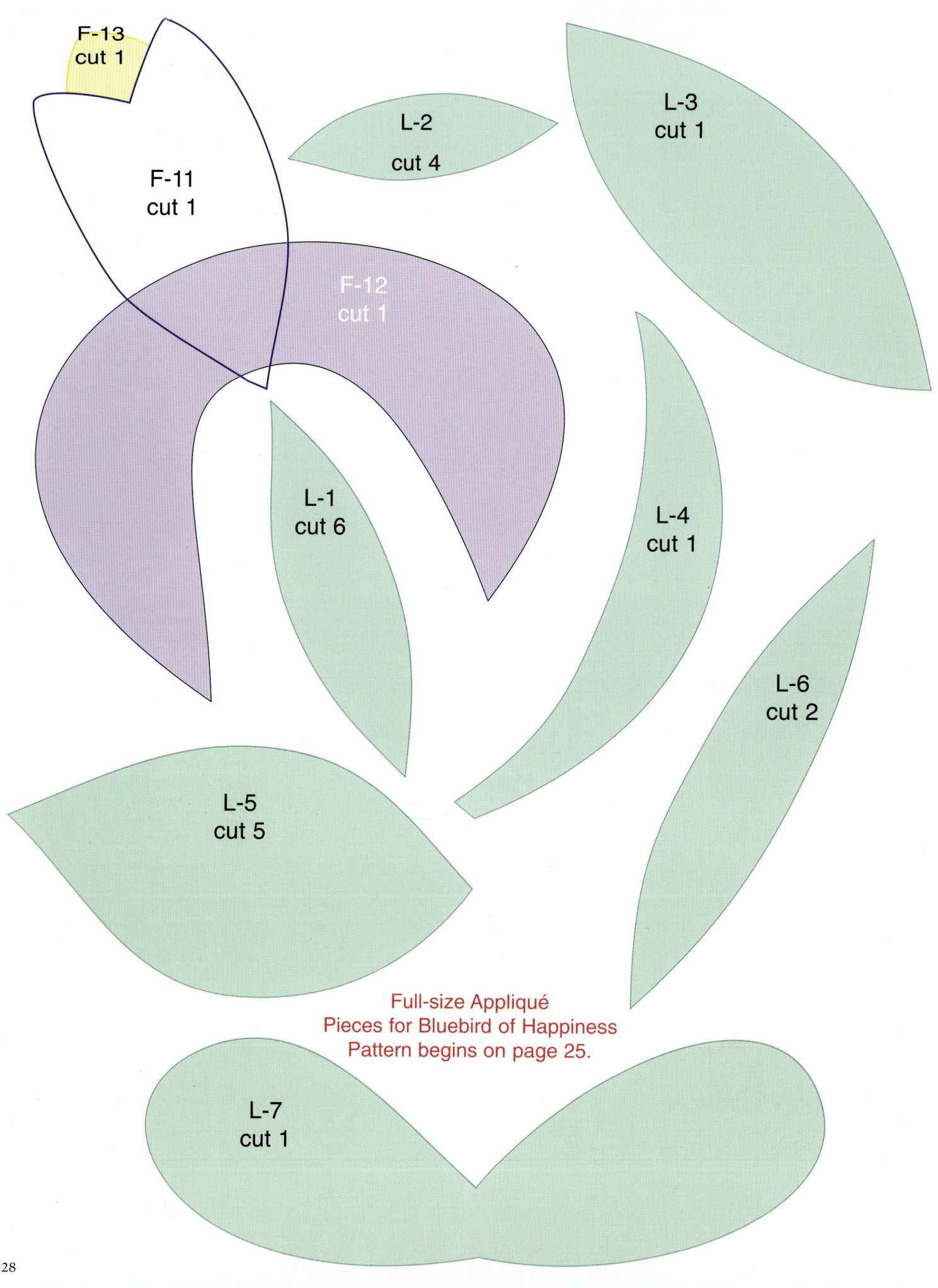

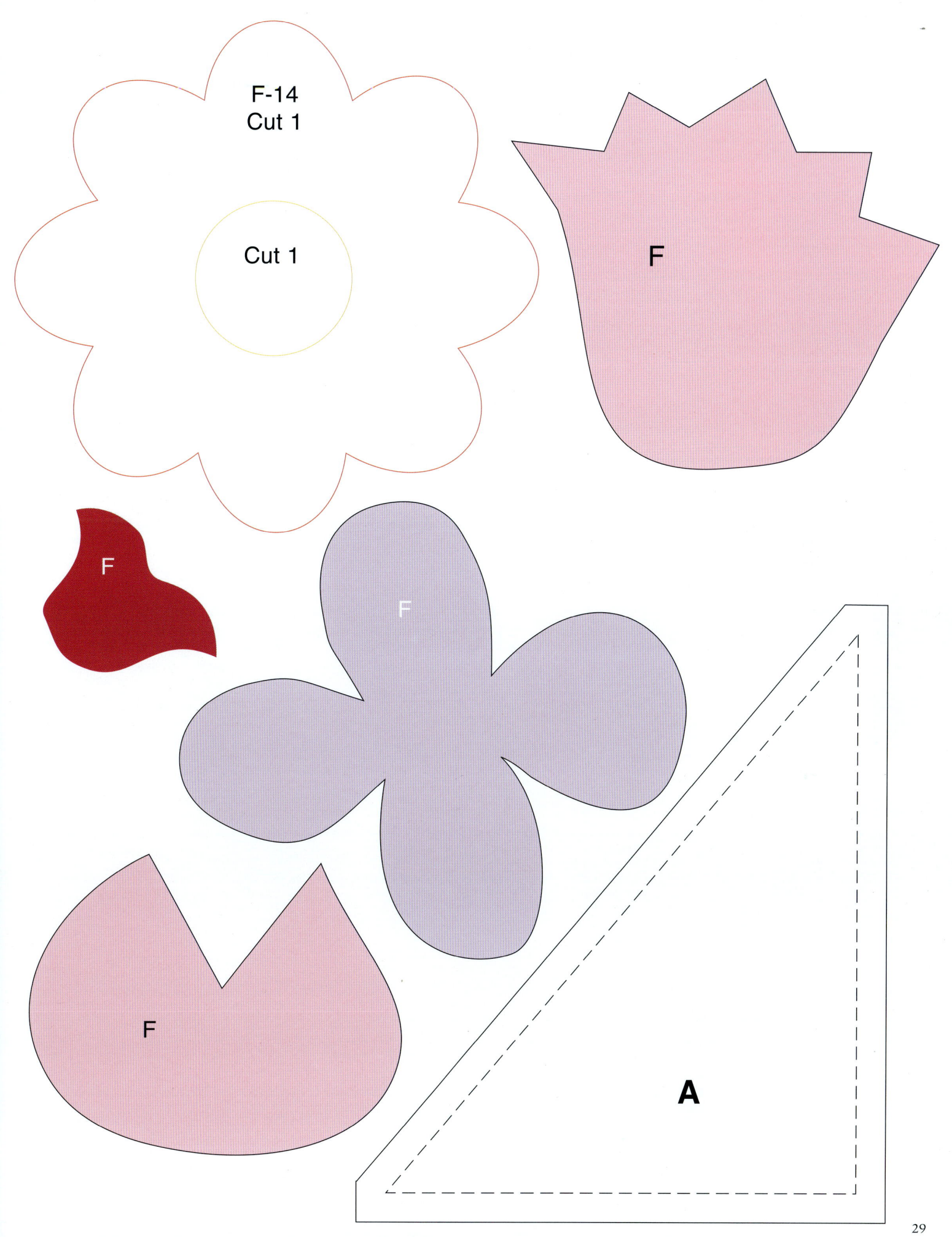

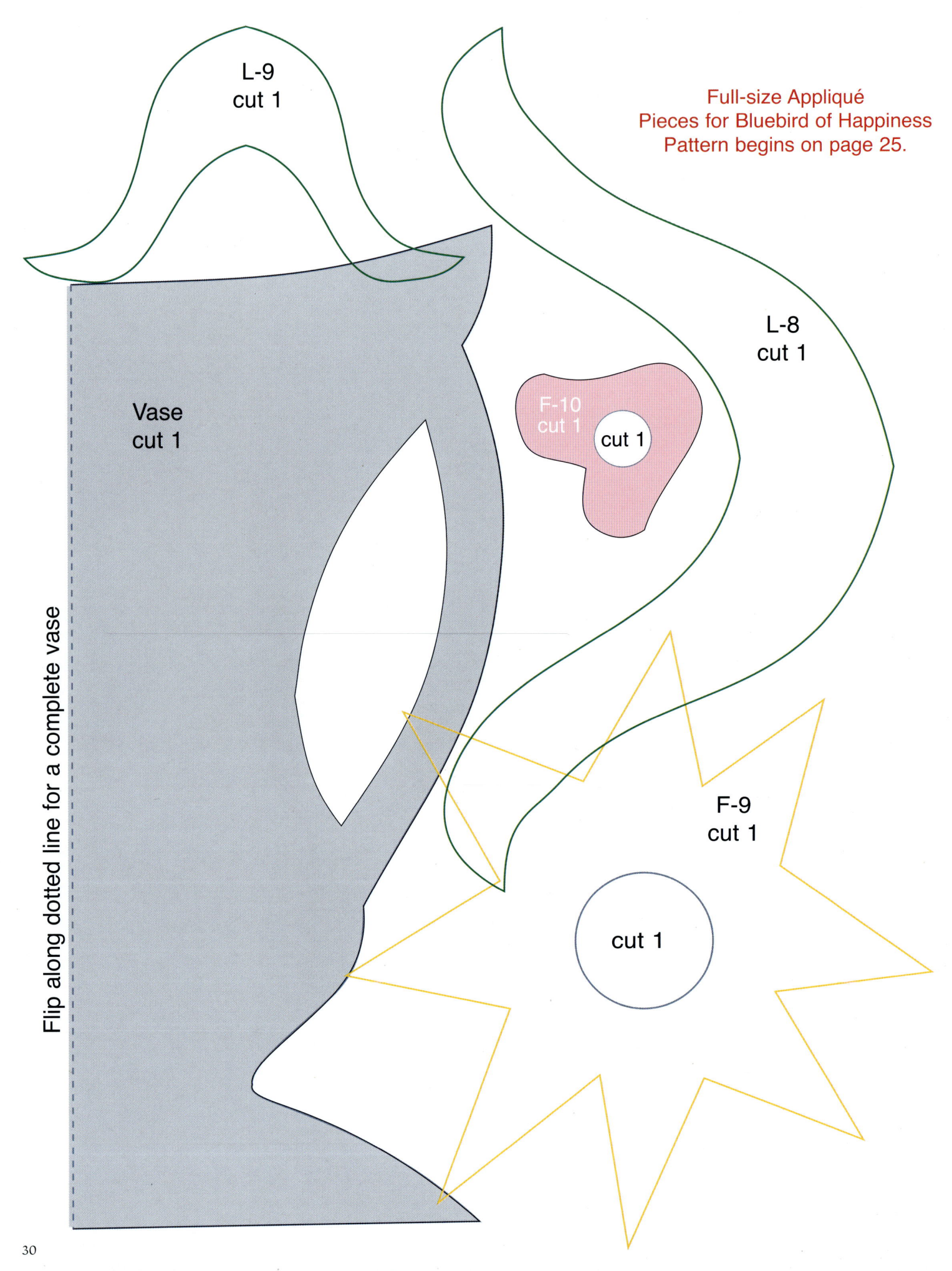

General Directions

CHOOSING A PATTERN

Read through all directions when choosing a pattern.

The pattern pieces are full size. Unless otherwise noted, all pieces include 1/4" seam allowances. The solid line is the cutting line and the dashed line is the stitching line.

An "R" means that you will need to reverse that pattern piece before tracing.

FABRIC

Yardage requirements are based on 44"-wide fabric. Listed amounts are adequate, but little is allowed for errors. We suggest using 100% cotton fabrics.

TEMPLATES

Firm, clear plastic is best for making templates. Place a sheet of template plastic over the pattern pieces and accurately trace the cutting line and/or stitching line for each piece.

NOTE: *Templates for machine piecing include a seam allowance. Templates for appliqué pieces usually do not include a seam allowance.* Use a permanent marker to record on every template the name and size of the block, the grainline and the number of pieces needed for one block.

MARKING FABRICS

There are many marking tools available. Select the type you like best, remembering to test for removability. Keep these pointers in mind when marking: 1) If using pencil, sharpen it often. 2) Line up the grainline on the template accurately with the grainline of the fabric. 3) Place a piece of fine sandpaper under the fabric to prevent slipping. 4) For hand piecing, mark the wrong side of the fabric and flip all directional (asymmetrical) templates before tracing them. 5) Mark and cut just enough pattern pieces to make a sample block. Piece the block to determine the accuracy of each template. 6) Handle bias edges with care to avoid stretching.

When marking fabric for appliqué, trace the templates on the right side of the fabric, placing the wrong side of the template against the right side of the fabric. Leave at least 3/16" around hand appliqué templates to allow for a turn-under allowance on each piece. If using the buttonhole stitch or machine appliqué techniques, cut directly on the traced line.

PIECING

For machine piecing, set the stitch length at 12 stitches per inch and make sure the seamline lies exactly 1/4" from the edge of the fabric. Mark the throat plate with a piece of masking tape placed 1/4" away from the point at which the needle pierces the fabric. Unless otherwise noted, backstitching is not necessary for machine piecing. Start and stop stitching at the cut edges of the pieces. For set-in pieces, start and stop stitching 1/4" from the edges of the piece, backstitching at both ends.

When many of the same pieced unit are required, chain piece them through the machine without stopping. Leave the presser foot down and set the pieces against one another. Clip the threads after all the pieces are stitched.

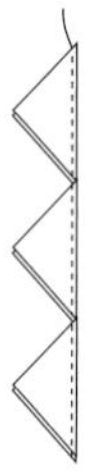

When hand piecing, begin with a small backstitch. Continue stitching with a small running stitch, taking one small backstitch every 3 or 4 stitches. Stitch directly on the seamlines of each piece, from point to point, rather than from cut edge to cut edge. Finish each seam with another small backstitch.

APPLIQUÉ

To hand appliqué, baste or pin appliqué pieces to the background fabric. Turn the raw edges of each appliqué piece under with the tip of the needle and take small hidden stitches to secure the piece to the background.

To machine appliqué, baste pieces in place with a long machine basting stitch or a narrow, open zigzag stitch. Then stitch over the basting with a short, wide satin stitch. Placing a piece of paper between the wrong side of the fabric and the feed dogs of the sewing machine will help stabilize the fabric. Carefully remove excess paper when stitching is complete.

FINISHING

Pressing

Press seam allowances to one side unless otherwise directed. Press with a dry iron to avoid stretching fabric. Whenever possible, press seam allowances toward the darker of the two pieces. Otherwise, press toward the lighter fabric and trim away 1/16" from the darker seam allowance. This will prevent the darker fabric from showing through the top of the quilt. Press all blocks, sashings and borders before assembling the quilt top.

Mitering Corners

For mitered borders, the pattern allows extra length on each border strip. Stitch each border to the quilt top, beginning, and backstitching each seamline 1/4" from the edge of the quilt top. After all borders have been attached in this manner, miter one corner at a time. With the quilt top lying right side down, lay one border over the other. Draw a straight line at a 45° angle from the inner corner to the outer corner, as shown.

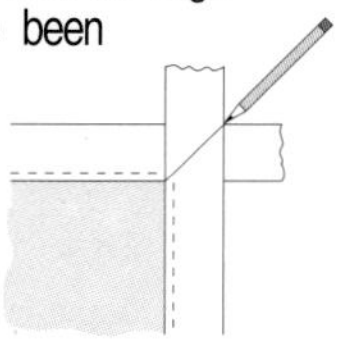

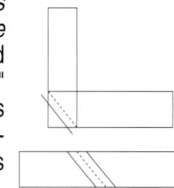

Reverse the positions of the borders and mark another straight line from corner to corner, in the same manner.

Place the borders, right sides together, with marked seamlines carefully matched and pinned and stitch from the outer to the inner corner backstitching at the inner corner. Open the mitered seam to make sure it lies flat, trim excess fabric and press.

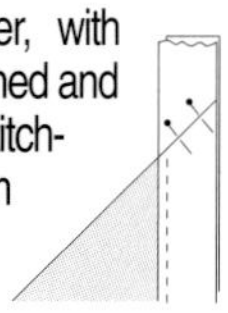

Marking Quilting Lines

Mark the lines for quilting before basting the quilt together with the batting and backing. We suggest using a very hard (#3 or #4) pencil or a chalk pencil (for darker fabrics) though many marking tools are available. Test any marking method to be sure that the lines will wash out and not damage the fabric in any way. Transfer paper quilting designs by placing fabric over the design and tracing. A light box or a brightly lit window may be necessary when using darker fabrics. Precut plastic stencils allow you to trace the quilting design onto the fabric from the front. Check to be sure they fit the area you wish to quilt. Use a ruler to keep lines straight and even when marking grid lines.

Some quilting may be done without marking the top at all. Outline quilting (1/4" from the seamline) or quilting "in the ditch" can be done "by eye." Quilting "in the ditch" is done next to the seam (but not through it) on the patch opposite the pressed seam allowances.

Other straight lines may also be marked as you quilt by using the edge of masking tape as a stitching guide. For simple quilting motifs (hearts, stars, etc.) cut the shape(s) from clear, sticky-back paper (such as Contact® Paper) and position them on your quilt top. These shapes can be reused many times. Do not leave masking tape or adhesive paper on your quilt top overnight. Remove it when you are finished quilting for the day to avoid leaving a residue.

Basting

Cut the batting and backing at least 2" larger than the quilt top on all sides. Place the backing, wrong side up, on a flat surface and anchor in place with masking tape, if possible. Smooth the batting over the backing. Smooth the quilt top, right side up, over the batting. Baste the three layers together with thread or safety pins to form a quilt "sandwich." Beginning at the center of the quilt, baste horizontally first and then vertically. Add additional horizontal and vertical lines of stitches or pins approximately every 6" until the entire top is held together securely. Quilt as desired.

Binding

After the basting is removed, trim excess batting and backing to within 1/4" of the quilt top.

For most straight-edged quilts, a double-fold French binding is an attractive, durable and easy finish. NOTE: *If your quilt has curved or scalloped edges, binding strips must be cut on the bias of the fabric.* To make 1/2" finished binding, cut each strip 2 1/2" wide. Sew binding strips (cross grain or bias) together with diagonal seams; trim and press seams open.

Fold the binding strip in half lengthwise, wrong sides together, and press. Position the binding strip on the right side of the quilt top, aligning the raw edges of the binding with the edge of the quilt top, (not so that all raw edges are even.) Leave approximately 6" of binding strip free. Beginning several inches from one corner, stitch the binding to the quilt with a 1/2" seam allowance measuring from the raw edge of the backing. When you reach a corner, stop the stitching line exactly 1/2" from the edge. Backstitch, clip threads and remove the quilt from the machine. Fold the binding up and away, creating a 45° angle, as shown.

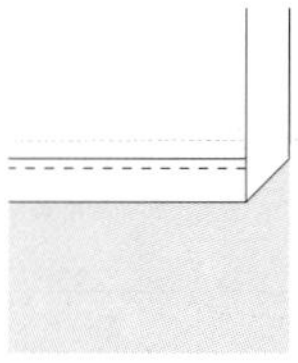

Keeping the angled folds secure, fold the binding back down. This fold should be even with the edge of the quilt top. Begin stitching at the fold.

Continue sewing the binding in this manner, stopping 6" from the starting point. To finish, fold both strips back along the edge of the quilt so that the folded edges meet about 3" from both lines of stitching and the binding lies flat on the quilt. Finger press to crease the folds. Cut both strips 1 1/4" from the folds.

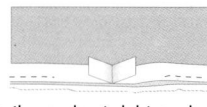

Open both strips and place the ends at right angles to each other, right sides together. Fold the bulk of the quilt out of your way. Join the strips with a diagonal seam, as shown.

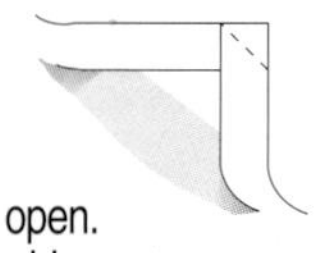

Trim the seam to 1/4" and press it open. Fold the joined strips so that wrong sides are together again. Place the binding flat against the quilt and finish stitching it to the quilt. Trim the layers as needed so that the binding edge will be filled with batting when you fold the binding to the back of the quilt. Blindstitch the binding to the back of the quilt, covering the seamline.

FINISHING THE QUILT

Remove any markings visible on the quilt top. Be sure to sign and date your quilt.